Science fair

NOV -- 2002
L I

Science Fair
Success

Science Fair Success with Scents, Aromas, and Smells

Thomas R. Rybolt

and

Leah M. Rybolt

Enslow Publishers, Inc.

40 Industrial Road	PO Box 38
Box 398	Aldershot
Berkeley Heights, NJ 07922	Hants GU12 6BP
USA	UK

http://www.enslow.com

This book is dedicated to my colleagues and friends in the Department of Chemistry at the University of Tennessee at Chattanooga who have made twenty years of teaching and research an enjoyable experience. —TR

Acknowledgments

We recognize the support provided by the William H. Wheeler Center for Odor Research at the University of Tennessee at Chattanooga. We thank Thomas A. Orofino, Ph.D., and Ann H. Rybolt, M.D., for their encouragement and helpful comments. Dr. Orofino's Wheeler Odor Research Reports provided additional useful information. Also, we thank John McLean, Ph.D., of Memorial University of Newfoundland and Mary Chisolm, Ph.D., of Pennsylvania State University at Erie for their review of the manuscript and helpful suggestions.

Library of Congress Cataloging-in-Publication Data

Rybolt, Thomas R.
    Science fair success with scents, aromas, and smells / Thomas R. Rybolt, Leah M. Rybolt.
        p. cm. — (Science fair success)
    Includes bibliography and index.
    ISBN 0-7660-1625-0
    1. Smell—Juvenile literature. 2. Science Projects—Juvenile literature. [1. Smell—Experiments. 2. Senses and sensation—Experiments. 3. Experiments. 4. Science projects.]
    I. Rybolt, Leah M. II. Title. III. Series.
    QP458 .R935   2002
    612.8'6'078—dc21

                            2001001780

Printed in the United States of America

10 9 8 7 6 5 4 3 2 1

To Our Readers:
We have done our best to make sure all Internet addresses in this book were active and appropriate when we went to press. However, the author and the publisher have no control over and assume no liability for the material available on those Internet sites or on other Web sites they may link to. Any comments or suggestions can be sent by e-mail to comments@enslow.com or to the address on the back cover.

Illustration Credits: Stephen F. Delisle

Cover Photo: © 1997–2000 Hemera Technologies, Inc.

Contents

Introduction

Have you noticed that wherever you go, your nose is out in front leading the way? What good is your nose, besides pointing you in the right direction or holding up a pair of glasses? Your nose helps you breathe and smell. This book is about the world of odors and the sense of smell—what goes on behind your nose, inside your head and brain.

Through your sense of smell, your brain is able to identify specific molecules floating in the air around you. Close your eyes, breathe deep, and sniff at the air. Do you smell a cup of coffee across the room, a peanut butter sandwich on the table, or someone's new perfume?

How does your brain tell you what is in the air around you when you cannot see, hear, or touch it? Why are people so concerned with getting rid of bad odors and finding good ones? How do plants and animals use smell? How can a simple scent trigger a memory you have not had in years? Why can you briefly smell a food and know you do not want to taste it? This book is a collection of simple yet sensational sensory experiments to help you learn the answers to these and other fantastic odor questions.

Scents—Big Business and New Knowledge

Industries around the world make products or use products to add, remove, control, and modify odors. If you walk through a grocery store, it is hard to find a food or product that does not have a smell associated with it. Many products have odors added to them—from lemon-scented dishwashing liquid to scented candles. Some stores have displays of aromatic oils used in aromatherapy. Worldwide, perfume is a 15-billion-dollar industry! On the other hand, people spend billions of dollars on products that remove or control bad odors. They use everything from room deodorizers to body deodorants.

In recent years, there has been an explosion of knowledge about odors and the sense of smell. More than a thousand different genes in human DNA are used to make protein receptors that allow people to smell thousands of types of molecules. Scientists have learned a great deal about how the sense of smell works. They have identified many specific odor compounds produced by plants, animals, and humans and how they affect behavior. New methods of insect control use chemicals called pheromones that attract insects into traps. Other chemical odors are used to attract or repel fish, birds, and other animals.

Even the Internet can be used for odors. DigiScents is a company that sends scents over the Internet. Actually, they sell a small device that attaches to a computer. This device contains different chemicals that can be released into the room to give a desired scent. If you are playing a computer game, you can smell what is going on at the same time you see and hear it. Or you could send someone a picture of roses and have a rose scent released at the same time. Maybe some day a company selling pizzas will let you smell the toppings you want—or *don't* want—before you order.

How to Use This Book

Each chapter in this book has an introduction to a topic, followed by four main experiments. Each experiment will expand your knowledge of the chapter topic. The experiments do not have to be done in any special order. You can also skip around in the book to find the chapters that interest you most. Read the chapter introductions before you perform the experiments.

A section at the beginning of each experiment lists the materials you will need. The materials are all common items that are in your home or for sale at a grocery store.

At the end of each experiment you will find a section called "Project Ideas and Further Investigations," which contains suggestions for additional experiments. You can use any of the original experiments or suggested further experiments as a great starting point to develop your own original science fair project.

You should use a science notebook when you are doing experiments. Any notebook with bound pages—such as a spiral notebook—will do. You should always record the date, a description of what you are doing, and all your data and observations. If you are working on a science fair project, your notebook will be an important source of information to show your teacher and judges the work you have done.

As you learn more about odor science, you will learn about many different sciences. Understanding the sense of smell involves biology, chemistry, physics, medicine, human physiology, animal behavior, psychology, and more. If you want to use this book to get a sense for scents, bring your nose along, and be ready to smell.

Safety

- Make sure an adult in your household knows what you are doing and has approved your activities.

- These experiments can be done in the kitchen at home or at school as a part of a science class or lab. Ask a parent, teacher, or other adult if you need help with any experiment.

- Clean up after each experiment is completed.

- Follow any special instructions given in the experiment or given on the label of any product you are using.

- **Warning:** If either you or a volunteer helping you suffers from allergies, migraine headaches triggered by odors, or asthma, do not use any foods or objects that can cause medical problems.

- **Warning:** Never smell hazardous products such as ammonia, bleach, gasoline, kerosene, or solvents. Do not breathe the fumes of other household products such as airplane glue, nail polish remover, or paint.

Chapter 1

Where Your Brain Meets the World of Scents

When you breathe, air enters your nostrils and goes into two nasal passageways, which lead up from the nose and then back down to the throat. Each nasal passage has thin bones called turbinates that direct the flow of air to the top of the nasal cavity. At the top of each nasal passage is a dime-sized spot called the olfactory epithelium. This spot is where your brain meets the world of scents. Here, special brain nerve cells called olfactory receptor neurons are directly exposed to the scents of the outside world. Molecules from the air touch these olfactory neurons and generate signals that the brain recognizes as specific odors.

The olfactory epithelium contains about 20 million olfactory receptor neurons (nerve cells). These millions of nerve cells are centered just below our eyes, behind the bridge of our nose (see Figure 1a). Each neuron has a highly branched end, called the dendrite, with many hairlike cilia. The dendrites are exposed to and detect odor molecules that dissolve in mucus around the cilia. A long portion of each neuron, called the axon, joins the axons of other olfactory receptor neurons to form olfactory nerves. These olfactory nerves go through the skull to connect with a brain structure called the olfactory bulb (see Figure 1b).

Special protein molecules help bind odor molecules and concentrate the odor. Odor molecules from the air go into the thick, slimy mucus that coats the olfactory receptor neurons. Then the odor molecules bind at receptor sites along the cilia at the ends of the olfactory receptor neurons. Just like a key fits into a lock or a ball into a glove, odor molecules from the air fit into these special sites called olfactory receptors (see Figure 1c).

Although there are many millions of olfactory receptors in a person's olfactory epithelium, there are only about a thousand types of receptors. Each of the millions of olfactory neurons has just one type of receptor on it so there are also about a thousand types of neurons. A specific type of odor molecule will partially fit into only some of the receptors. All the neurons that have a partial fit with a certain type of odor molecule will send electric nerve signals along their axons to structures called glomeruli in the olfactory bulb. This unique pattern of signals from selected neurons is different from what would be generated by a different type of molecule. The brain interprets each signal pattern as a specific smell.

The vomeronasal organ provides another way to sense or smell molecules that are important in controlling animal behavior. These signals go directly to a different olfactory bulb

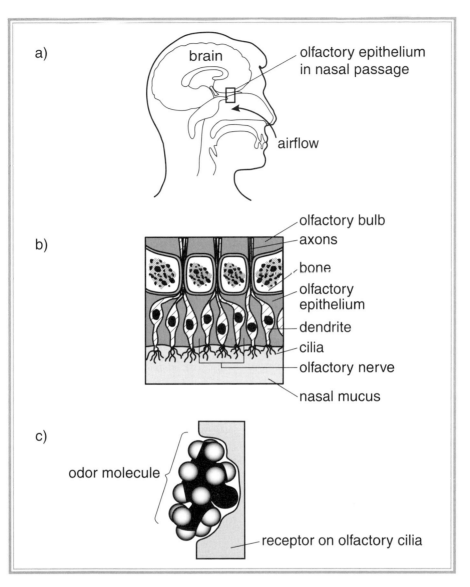

a) brain — olfactory epithelium in nasal passage

airflow

b) olfactory bulb
axons
bone
olfactory epithelium
dendrite
cilia
olfactory nerve
nasal mucus

c) odor molecule

receptor on olfactory cilia

Figure 1. a) The olfactory epithelium is at the top of each nasal passage. b) The olfactory epithelium is lined with special nerve cells whose branched dendrite ends are covered with cilia and bathed with mucus. The long axons of the olfactory receptor neurons extend through the skull into the olfactory bulb. c) The tiny cilia contain olfactory protein receptor sites into which selected odor molecules can fit and trigger electric impulses. The olfactory bulb receives these nerve impulses, organizes them, and allows the brain to interpret specific molecules as having unique odors.

and to a brain structure that controls instinctive behavior. This other sense of smell is essential for some survival activities, like animal mating.

Where the world of scent touches the brain, people's lives are made richer. They are protected from danger by smelling smoke or spoiled food. They remember their past through the scent of flowers or a favorite perfume. They enjoy the aromas of cooking food and taste the flavor of food mostly through smell. The olfactory epithelium is continuously bathed by an incredible mixture of ever-changing molecules. As these molecules bind to receptor sites on olfactory neurons, electrical signals are sent to the olfactory bulb and brain. These signals are the smells of the world.

This first chapter investigates some of the basics of the sense of smell—how people identify, distinguish, and locate odors, and their sensitivity to scents.

Experiment 1.1

Identifying Objects by Odor

Identifying objects by the way they smell is important to the survival of many animals. Sharks follow the smell of blood to find injured prey. Salmon, in preparation to reproduce, use smell to help them return to the same river where they were born. Badgers use their keen sense of smell to find and eat hundreds of worms in just a few hours. Humans

Materials

* ✱ 10 household items, such as butter, chocolate, plain soap, orange juice, coffee, piece of newspaper, lettuce, ketchup, apple, perfume
* ✱ 10 clean spoons
* ✱ 5 or more volunteers

cannot smell worms in the ground, but in this experiment you will learn something about what kinds of odors people can recognize.

Find small amounts of the ten household items listed as materials. If you do not have all of these items, you may find others to replace them. Put a small amount of each item onto a separate spoon. Perfume can be left in its bottle. List the ten items you are using in your science notebook. Leave plenty of room below each item for notes.

Have the first volunteer sit in a room where he cannot see or smell any of the test items. Ask this volunteer to close his eyes and keep them closed. One at a time, bring in a spoon with an item to be smelled. Do not let your hand get too close to the volunteer's nose because it could confuse the smell. Hold the spoon under the volunteer's nose (see Figure 2a), and ask him to smell the spoon for about five seconds. Ask him what he smells. Record his answer below the item name in your notebook. Continue until all ten objects have been tested.

Repeat this experiment with additional volunteers. In your science notebook, record the answers from each volunteer. When you have all the data recorded from each volunteer, compare their answers.

How many items did each volunteer correctly identify? Did your volunteers recognize as many odors as you thought they would? Did certain objects have odors that were commonly confused with something else? For example, soap can have many different odors added to it. What were the most difficult and what were the easiest odors to recognize? Make a chart that shows how many of your volunteers correctly identified each odor (see Figure 2b).

Was it easier for volunteers to correctly identify the smell of objects they have been around more often? Compare the results of different volunteers. Are some people better at recognizing smells than others? If any volunteers had a cold or stuffy nose, did they have trouble recognizing smells?

When an odor signal reaches the brain, there are qualities of the odor that may make it easier to identify. If it is a unique odor with a distinct smell, the brain will have an easier time distinguishing it. If the odor is one that the person commonly smells, the person will have a strong memory of that smell, so it will be easier for the person to remember the odor.

Scientists believe humans can distinguish between as many as ten thousand different odors. Distinguishing between odors means you can tell that one odor is different from another,

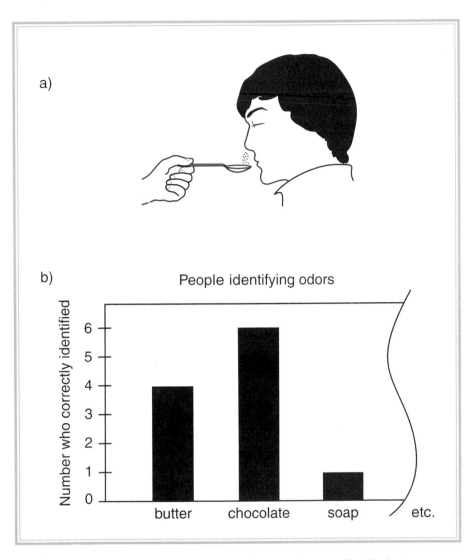

Figure 2. a) Can your volunteers identify what they smell with their eyes closed? b) Put the results of your smell experiment in a chart to show how many people correctly identified each odor.

even though you cannot identify it by name. Identifying an odor is more difficult than distinguishing between odors. To identify a smell, your brain must know the name of the odor, not just recognize that it is different from another odor. Although people can distinguish between thousands of different smells, most people can identify and name only about one hundred to three hundred specific odors. However, there are some people who have trained their sense of smell to recognize and identify thousands of odors. Some of these people use their highly trained sense of smell for identifying and preparing the complicated mixtures that make perfumes.

Project Ideas and Further Investigations

- Try increasing the number of objects to smell. Include common materials, such as toothpaste, deodorant, pizza, popcorn, cheese, lemon, lemon-scented soap, carrot, mustard, and milk. Which items are easiest to identify by smell and which ones are most difficult? Are items with added perfumes—such as toothpaste and deodorant—harder to identify? Based on the original experiment, can you predict which objects the most people will recognize?
- Try giving the volunteers less time to smell each object. Does it make identification harder, or is it the same as long as they get one good sniff?

Experiment 1.2

Distinguishing Mixtures

Materials

* mustard
* piece of chocolate
* stick of cinnamon chewing gum
* 7 clean spoons
* partner

In Experiment 1.1 you learned that people are able to recognize many specific foods or objects by using their sense of smell. But do you think people can distinguish between two or three different odors simultaneously?

First, you will need to prepare 7 different spoons with the items to be tested. Put similar amounts of each item in the spoons following these directions: spoon 1, chocolate; spoon 2, cinnamon gum; spoon 3, mustard; spoon 4, chocolate and cinnamon gum; spoon 5, chocolate and mustard; spoon 6, cinnamon gum and mustard; and spoon 7, chocolate, cinnamon gum, and mustard (see Figure 3). In spoons with two or three items, set the items side-by-side in the spoon. Do not cover one item with another.

Allow your partner to look at the spoons so she knows the possible combinations. However, keep the spoons far enough away so your partner cannot smell them.

In your science notebook, make a column listing the 7 spoons and what they contain. Have your partner close her eyes and keep them closed. Select one spoon and hold it under your partner's nose. Allow her to take just one quick sniff and then ask her what she smelled. Repeat this procedure for all the spoons and be sure to record each answer. Do not test th

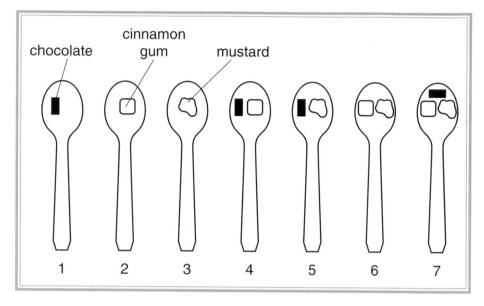

Figure 3. You need to prepare spoons with odor samples containing the following: spoon 1, chocolate; spoon 2, cinnamon gum; spoon 3, mustard; spoon 4, chocolate and cinnamon gum; spoon 5, chocolate and mustard; spoon 6, cinnamon gum and mustard; and spoon 7, chocolate, cinnamon gum, and mustard.

spoons in order from 1 to 7, but instead change the order around. Also, you can use the same spoon more than once and see whether the odors are identified the same way each time.

After you have finished testing your partner, trade places. Smell each spoon with your eyes closed. You may want to repeat the experiment several times.

You and your partner were probably easily able to identify the chocolate, cinnamon, and mustard when they were not mixed with anything else. Each of these items has a distinctive odor. When they were mixed two at a time, you still may have been able to identify the two items. However, people usually cannot pick out and identify three separate odors at the same time.

You know that you can look at a table and identify many objects at once. Does it surprise you that your sense of smell is so different from your sense of vision? Can you think of ways that your sense of smell is more like vision or more like hearing?

Odors blend together like several notes played on a piano all at once. You can smell the blended odors just as you can hear blended music. A meal of different foods or even just one food item can consist of many different odor molecules blended together. However, just as you may not be able to separate out the individual notes in a song, you cannot identify at once all the unique odors in a complex mixture.

Olfactory receptor neurons have about a thousand different kinds of receptor sites (and millions of individual receptors) where specific parts of molecules fit and bind. A collection of one kind of molecule may fit into several specific types of sites and thus activate signals from several different types of receptors. Just like a combination of letters is used to make a word, a combination of activated receptors is used to identify a specific odor. However, because many different types of receptors could be activated, a person's brain cannot sort out and separate all the signals from several different types of molecules at once. People recognize the odor blend, but cannot identify every unique odor molecule.

Project Ideas and Further Investigations

- Try repeating this experiment but give your partner as long as she wants to try to identify the mixed odors. You may find that when a person has longer to concentrate, she is able to pick out first one odor and then the second and then the third. With continued sniffing, the brain may be able to distinguish each of three mixed odors but only by identifying them one at a time. Some professional perfumers have trained their sense of smell to be able to sort out different odors from a complex mixture.

- Try using various combinations of foods and other smelly objects. Test as many different people as you can. Are some odor combinations more difficult to sort out because they smell so similar? Can you find other combinations of odors that are much easier to distinguish?

Experiment 1.3

Location by Nose

Some dogs are trained to sniff out
explosives and drugs. Other dogs are
used to track criminals or to locate
people that are lost in the wilderness.
Do you think that you could find a
hidden scent, like a dog can? In this
activity, you will find out.

Materials

* 10 index cards

* peppermint extract

* pencil

* paper towel

* partner

Write the word PEPPERMINT
lightly in pencil on one side of an
index card. Hold this side of the card tightly against the top of
an open bottle of peppermint extract. Turn the bottle of peppermint upside down while holding the card in place. Wait
until the liquid has spread onto the card to make a spot about
the size of a quarter. Turn the bottle over and remove the card.
Put the top back on the bottle.

Set the card on a paper towel. Wash your hands to remove
any peppermint odor. Keep the other 9 index cards separate
from the peppermint-scented card. You do not want the odor
to get onto the other cards.

Peppermint extract contains alcohol, water, and peppermint oil. (Peppermint oil comes from a plant in the mint
family.) The alcohol and water will evaporate and leave the
peppermint oil on the card. Wait about 30 minutes to be sure
the peppermint card is dry.

While you have your eyes closed, have your partner arrange
the 10 cards in a line along the edge of a clean table. Your partner should make sure the word PEPPERMINT is facing do

you cannot see which card it is. Open your eyes, and sit in front of the cards. Move your nose along the row of cards, sniffing each one (see Figure 4). Try to find the peppermint-scented card. After you are certain you have located the smelly card, turn it over. Were you correct?

Before you repeat the experiment, make sure the peppermint odor has not gotten on the table from the odor card. If you can smell peppermint on the table, you will need to put some paper towels under the cards, and change the paper before each experiment.

Humans mostly depend on their senses of sight and hearing to perceive the world. However, dogs and other animals are very dependent on their sense of smell. Dogs have about fifteen times more area for olfactory cells than humans do. A dog has about 200 million olfactory receptor cells in its nasal

Figure 4. Just as a dog can track a scent, you can try to find which card contains peppermint by using your sense of smell.

passages. A large part of a dog's brain is used to identify odors. Pads on their paws leave scent trails, and dogs use their urine to mark their territory. Dogs perceive a rich and complex world of scents and smells that humans can only imagine.

Because dogs have such a keen sense of smell, they can be trained to track humans or identify hidden substances like drugs and explosives. Although your sense of smell will never match a dog's ability, you can locate some objects by smell.

Project Ideas and Further Investigations

- Try using other odors on the cards or using a mixture of odors. Are some odors easier to locate than others? Does a mixture of odors make it harder or easier to pick out one specific smell?
- After what period of time can a person still find the right card? Without adding any more peppermint, repeat the experiment after 1 hour, 3 hours, 6 hours, 1 day, 2 days, or more. Compare how often people can find the peppermint card after different lengths of time. Peppermint can still be present after some time, but may be below the threshold that people can detect (see Experiment 1.4).

23

Experiment 1.4

Odor Threshold

Your nasal odor receptors and olfactory bulb may not be able to pick up the smell of a single molecule of limonene found in lemon juice. However, they would be able to sense the odor of a whole bottle of lemon juice and many limonene molecules. Whether someone is able to smell an odor depends on how much of the odor is present and how many other odors are also in the air. In this experiment, you will test your volunteers' odor threshold of tea.

A threshold is the point at which a mental or physical effect begins to

Materials

* 5 empty glass jars
* tea bag
* water
* spoon
* microwave oven
* an adult
* measuring container or separate cups with marks at 1/4 , 1/2 , 3/4, and 1 cup
* microwave-safe coffee mug
* 3 volunteers

take place. In the sense of smell, the threshold is the number of odor molecules needed in the air for the odor to be detected. The absolute threshold is the smallest detectable amount of odor molecules. For example, humans are quite sensitive to the odor of sulfur-containing compounds. Hydrogen sulfide (H_2S) is a compound given off by rotten eggs and can be poisonous in excessive amounts. People can detect less than 1 gram of hydrogen sulfide even if it is mixed with 10 billion grams of air!

In this experiment, you will dissolve tea in water to reach the absolute threshold of the tea odor. In other words, you will find how much more water than tea there has to be before the smell of tea can no longer be detected.

To begin, **ask an adult** to place 1 cup of water in a microwave-safe coffee mug and heat it in a microwave oven for about 2 minutes. Be careful not to burn yourself; the water will be very hot. Put a tea bag in the coffee mug. Wait 3 minutes for the tea to dissolve in the water. After 3 minutes, remove the tea bag and stir the tea.

Measure out 1/4 cup of tea and pour it into a clear jar. Then add 3/4 cup of water into the same jar. This is a 1/4 dilution of the original tea. In the remaining four jars you will be diluting the tea more and more.

To make the remaining dilutions, first pour 1/2 cup of the tea dilution out of the first jar and put it in the second jar. Now add 1/2 cup of water into the second jar. Take 1/2 cup of the mixture in the second jar, and pour it into the third jar. Add 1/2 cup of water to the third jar. Now take 1/2 cup out of the third jar and pour it into the fourth jar. Then add 1/2 cup of water to the mixture in the fourth jar. Last, pour 1/2 cup from the fourth jar into the fifth jar, and add 1/2 cup of water to the fifth jar. Pour 1/2 cup of the mixture in the fifth jar down the sink.

Now you should have the same amount of liquid in each jar. The color of the tea should get lighter as you go from the first to the fifth jar. The amount of the original tea in each jar is: jar 1, 1/4; jar 2, 1/8; jar 3, 1/16, jar 4, 1/32; and jar 5, 1/64.

In your science notebook set up a chart to record your observations (see Figure 5). Have each volunteer first smell the tea in the coffee mug so he knows the aroma of tea. Then have him start with the first jar and move to the fifth. Ask him to smell each jar, and record whether he can smell any tea. Repeat this process with each volunteer, and finally smell each dilution yourself. Record the results in your chart.

Did all of you have the same absolute threshold for tea odor? Did some people stop smelling tea earlier than others? Could you see the tea even when you couldn't smell it?

RESULTS OF ODOR THRESHOLD DETECTION				
JAR	TEA DILUTION	VOLUNTEER 1: SMELLED TEA?	VOLUNTEER 2: SMELLED TEA?	VOLUNTEER 3: SMELLED TEA?
1	1/4	YES	YES	YES
2	1/8	YES	YES	YES
3	1/16	YES	YES	YES
4	1/32	NO	YES	NO
5	1/64	NO	NO	NO

Figure 5. You can prepare charts like this to compare the odor thresholds of different volunteers smelling diluted tea.

Project Ideas and Further Investigations

- Repeat the experiment with people of all ages—children, teenagers, and adults. Does age affect odor threshold? The sense of smell often declines in adults over 70, but very young children have not had as much experience in identifying odors. Can you explain any differences you find?
- Repeat the experiment again, but smell the fifth jar first and then go toward the more concentrated solutions. Do the results change when you start with the most diluted solution and go to the most concentrated? When humans smell a strong odor, they become less sensitive to smaller amounts of the same odor. Starting with a weaker odor may allow a person to sense more diluted concentrations of tea than in the first experiment.
- Repeat the experiment again, but smell the jars in a random order. Do the results change?

Chapter 2

Marvelous Moving Molecules

Wherever you are, molecules surround you. Molecules are groups of atoms bound together. Some of these molecules are familiar to you, but others may seem strange and mysterious. You may be familiar with molecules such as water (H_2O), carbon dioxide (CO_2), or natural gas (methane, or CH_4). You drink H_2O in a glass of water, you exhale CO_2 in every breath, and CH_4 may be piped into your home for heating or cooking.

In every cell of your body there are tens of thousands of different types of molecules that keep the cells alive and functioning. You are made of molecules. The most common molecule in your body is water. Water molecules are tiny. Just one drop of water could hold 2 million quadrillion (2,000,000,000,000,000,000,000) H_2O molecules.

Molecules in solids are locked in place, like the sucrose molecules ($C_{12}H_{22}O_{11}$) that pack together to make solid crystals of table sugar. Other molecules may slide past each other, like the H_2O molecules in a glass of water. However, in a gas, molecules are moving wildly about and constantly bumping into the other moving molecules around them.

It is only when molecules are in this wildly moving gas state that we can smell them. You do not smell a bowl of sugar that is on the table in front of you, because the sucrose molecules remain locked together as a solid. The molecules cannot reach your nose. However, if you have a bottle of perfume in front of you, some of the molecules will leave the liquid, go into the air, and eventually make it to your nose. Then they can be sniffed into your nasal passages. A volatile liquid is one in which at least some of the molecules will leave the liquid and become a gas. You can smell volatile liquids.

Molecules are collections of atoms that are held together by bonds between the atoms. These bonds are formed by sharing pairs of electrons. Positive protons and neutral neutrons are particles found in the tiny center, or nucleus, of each atom. Electrons around the nucleus give atoms their size. The protons and neutrons give atoms most of their mass.

Writing H_2O for water means that each water molecule is made of 2 hydrogen atoms and 1 oxygen atom. CH_4 contains 1 carbon and 4 hydrogen atoms in each molecule, and $C_5H_{12}S$ contains 5 carbon, 12 hydrogen, and 1 sulfur atom in each molecule.

$C_5H_{12}S$ is an interesting molecule with the tongue-twisting name 3-methylbutane-1-thiol. Striped skunks have anal sacs where this special molecule is stored. When the skunk is frightened, it can lift its tail and spray liquid containing this molecule at a person or threatening animal. These sulfur-containing molecules smell so bad that a person or animal that detects it will run away from the skunk. If you were to get sprayed, no one would want to get close to you. You would stink.

In this chapter, you will not experiment with $C_5H_{12}S$, but you will be exposed to some of the properties of other marvelous moving molecules.

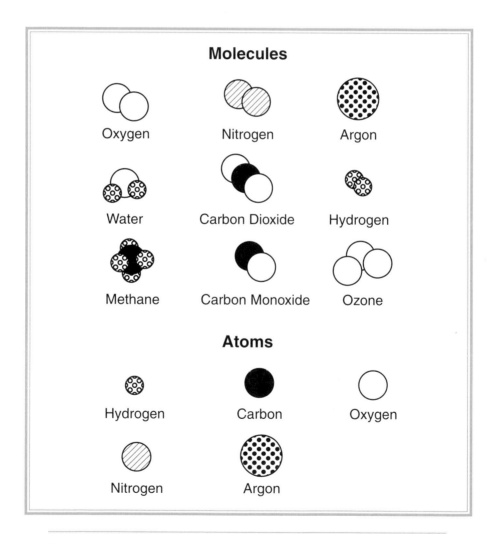

Experiment 2.1

Temperature and Odors

Have you ever been drawn to the kitchen by the aroma of cooking food? Do you get the same delightful smell of food when you open the freezer or take leftovers out of the refrigerator? Why do you think food smells different at different temperatures?

Materials

* 3 glass jars
* tea bag
* water
* measuring cup
* microwave oven
* an adult
* microwave-safe coffee mug

To begin this experiment, **ask an adult** to place about a cup of water in a microwave-safe coffee mug. Heat this water in a microwave oven for about 2 minutes. Place a tea bag in the coffee mug. Wait about 3 minutes, and then remove the tea bag.

Now pour 1/3 cup of tea into each jar. Place one jar in the freezer, and leave the others at room temperature. Wait 1 hour, and then remove the jar of tea from the freezer. Place one of the jars that had been sitting out into the microwave. Heat this jar of tea for 30 seconds. Carefully remove the hot jar from the microwave.

You should now have three jars of tea—one frozen, one at room temperature, and one hot (see Figure 6). Smell each jar of tea. Which tea smells the strongest, second strongest, and weakest? Can you explain why three jars of the same tea might smell different?

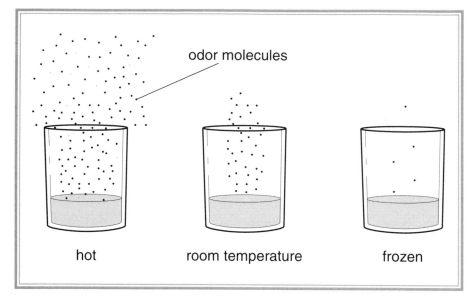

odor molecules

hot   room temperature   frozen

Figure 6. Odor molecules move faster and spread into the air quicker if they come from hot tea.

As you probably discovered, temperature affects how strong the tea smells. When the tea was heated in the microwave, it caused the molecules in the tea to move faster. The freezer had the opposite effect, causing the molecules in the tea to move slower. Slow-moving molecules leave a solid slowly. Fewer reach your nose, so the smell is not as strong. Faster-moving molecules are able to leave a hot liquid in greater numbers and get to your nose more quickly. More odor molecules cause a stronger smell. Rising steam also helps carry odor molecules from the hot tea to your nose.

Project Idea and Further Investigation

Before a meal is cooked, smell it; then smell it again after it is cooked. Does heat affect the odor of your meal the same way it affected the odor of the tea? In addition to heating molecules, cooking can also cause chemical reactions to occur. These chemical reactions cause new molecules to form that are responsible for aromas and flavors (see Experiment 3.2). Try comparing the smell of many different foods when they are frozen, at room temperature, and hot after cooking. Get volunteers to smell and then evaluate the strength of the odors and describe what they smell. Make a chart of different foods and analyze your results.

Experiment 2.2

Separating Scents

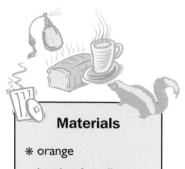

Perfumes, flower scents, and other complicated smells are often caused by a mixture of many molecules. How do scientists sort out the different parts of such complex mixtures? In this activity you will explore a way to separate a mixture into two different scents.

Materials

✳ orange

✳ bottle of vanilla extract

✳ paper towel

✳ drinking glass

✳ water

✳ small kitchen knife

✳ scissors

Remove several large pieces of peel from an orange. Make sure that the peel does not have any of the juicy part of the orange still attached.

When you squeeze a piece of orange peel, liquid squirts out. The liquid that comes from the outside of the peel contains a molecule called limonene. Limonene contributes to the smell found in citrus fruit, such as lemons and oranges. Squeeze a piece of orange peel and collect the liquid that comes out. Smell the liquid. Do you recognize the smell of limonene? In fact, orange oil contains other odor molecules besides limonene, but we will just refer to the limonene molecule here.

Vanilla extract contains vanillin molecules dissolved in a mixture of water and alcohol. Vanillin molecules mixed with alcohol will dissolve, or go into water. Smell the vanilla extract so you can recognize the smell of vanillin.

Cut a paper towel into a strip that is about 2.5 cm (1 in) and about 30.5 cm (12 in) long. Lay this paper-towel strip on a plate. Now squeeze the orange peel so that orange-oil liquid with limonene goes on the paper towel about 10 cm (4 in) from the end of the strip. Touch the peel to the paper towel to help transfer limonene liquid from the peel to the paper. Use 2 or 3 pieces of orange peel until the paper towel has a wet spot about the size of a quarter. Sniff this wet spot. Can you smell the orange oil containing limonene?

Next, add a few drops of vanilla extract to the limonene spot on the paper towel. Try to add about the same amount of vanilla extract as you added orange-peel liquid. Smell the wet spot on the paper towel. Hold the paper strip under your nose and close your eyes. Move the piece of paper towel back and forth under your nose. Can you use your sense of smell to locate the wet spot on the paper towel? Do you smell limonene or vanillin? The limonene may mask or cover up the smell of the vanillin.

Fill a glass with water. Make sure the outside of the glass is dry. Set the glass on the edge of a sink or table. Place the end of the paper towel nearer the odor spot into the glass of water. Let the rest of the strip, including the odor spot, hang over the glass (see Figure 7).

Watch as the paper towel absorbs water. Do you see water flow up the paper towel, over the edge of the glass, and down the length of the paper towel? Watch until water is dripping off the end of the paper towel that is not in the glass. Depending on the type of paper towel, it could take as long as 10 minutes for the water to get to the end. After water is dripping off the end of the paper towel, wait another couple of minutes and remove the paper strip from the glass. Carefully lay the wet strip on a dry paper towel.

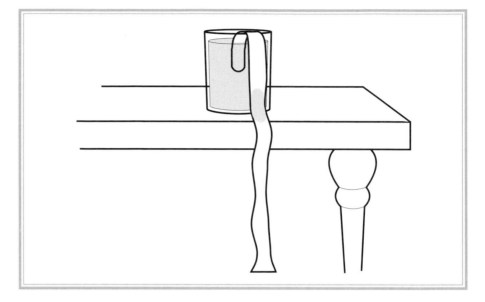

Figure 7. You can use water spreading down a strip of paper towel to do chromatography and separate a mixture of odors into separate scents.

Wait about 20 minutes until the strip is dry. Pick up the strip and move it back and forth under your nose. Do you smell limonene? If so, where? Do you smell vanillin? If so, where?

Were you able to separate the mixture of limonene and vanillin? Did the limonene move down the strip with the flowing water or stay in place? Did the vanillin move down the strip or stay in place?

Vanillin's molecular formula can be written as $C_8H_8O_3$. Vanillin occurs naturally in vanilla beans or can be made from wood pulp waste that contains lignin—a component of wood. Vanillin is somewhat soluble, meaning it will dissolve in an excess of water. Limonene is a molecule whose chemical formula can be written as $C_{10}H_{16}$. Limonene is a liquid that does not dissolve in water.

Chromatography is an important method used to separate mixtures of different molecules. A mixture is allowed to adsorb, or stick, on a solid. A liquid solvent, or a moving gas, flows through the solid adsorbent and carries molecules with it. Some molecules move with the solvent or gas and some tend to stay on the solid. In this way, molecules of different kinds are separated.

In your chromatography experiment, the paper towel was the solid and the water from the glass was the moving solvent. Limonene does not dissolve in water and so it tends to stay in place on the paper. Vanillin will dissolve somewhat so it is expected to move with the water. Did your results fit this prediction?

Project Ideas and Further Investigations

- Make a chart of how far limonene and vanillin move after 2, 4, 6, 8, and 10 minutes. At shorter times, the water may not make it to the end of the paper towel so you would expect the molecules to be less separated.
- Investigate other odor mixtures. Can you separate and detect other mixtures? Do some mixtures move with the water through the paper towel and thus stay together? Do some mixtures both remain in place and thus stay together?

Experiment 2.3

The Speed of Odor

The molecules in air are in constant, random motion. These molecules travel at speeds of hundreds of miles per hour. They bump into billions of other molecules every second. Because there are so many molecules that are moving so fast, each molecule only goes a short distance before it hits another molecule. Every time one molecule hits another molecule they both change directions. Imagine what happens when two moving billiard balls collide. Now imagine billions of such collisions happening every second. Molecules are like tiny billiard balls that are constantly moving.

> **Materials**
>
> * ruler
> * orange juice
> * measuring cup
> * aluminum foil
> * watch with timer or stopwatch
> * empty plastic 2-liter soda bottle
> * 2 volunteers

In this experiment, you will investigate how long it takes odor molecules to fight their way through all these collisions to reach your nose. After the odor molecules reach your nose, they can be sniffed into your nasal cavity. Then the odor molecules reach your olfactory epithelium where they are detected.

Rinse out an empty plastic 2-liter soda bottle. Pour 1/2 cup of orange juice into the clean, empty bottle. Shape a piece of aluminum foil into a small cap that can be placed over the bottle to seal it shut. When not in use, keep the bottle covered with this aluminum foil cap.

Have one volunteer hold a ruler vertical and next to his face so it measures the distance from his nostrils to the bottle.

This volunteer should close his eyes after the ruler is in place. Swirl the orange juice around the bottle and remove the aluminum cap. Immediately move the open bottle so its top is at the 3-cm mark on the ruler (see Figure 8) and say "start." When the volunteer who is holding the ruler first smells the orange juice have him say "stop." The other volunteer should start the timer when you say start, and stop it when the person smelling says stop. Move the bottle away from your volunteer and cover the bottle top after each timing.

Repeat this timing procedure at distances of 6, 9, 12, and 15 cm. Repeat all 5 distances at least three times, but do them in a random order. Make sure the orange juice odor is gone prior to repeating each timing experiment. Record all these times in a chart. List the distance the molecules traveled from

Figure 8. You can time how long it takes molecules to travel from a bottle through the air and into your nose where they finally reach your olfactory epithelium and are detected by your brain as a smell.

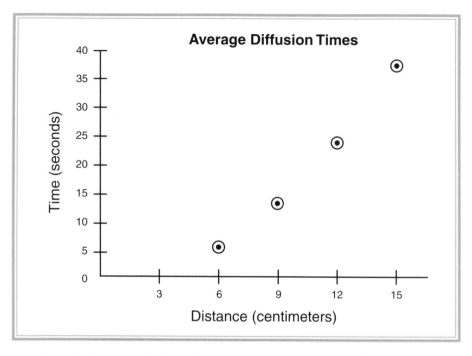

Figure 9. The graph shows the relationship between the distance odor molecules have to travel to reach your nose and the time required for them to be detected as a smell.

the bottle to your volunteer's nose. Record the times next to the distance traveled.

Average the times for each distance and make a plot of average time (y-axis) versus distance (x-axis). Do you find that your data points give a curve (see Figure 9) indicating that as distance increases, the time to diffuse also increases?

The spreading of a collection of gaseous molecules is called diffusion. The mixture of molecules that give the odor of orange juice have to diffuse through the air from the top of the bottle to your volunteer's nose. Does it make sense that the farther the molecules have to go, the longer it takes them to get there?

Project Ideas and Further Investigations

- Repeat this experiment with different volunteers and compare the times people report to smell the odors. Are the numbers the same from one person to another or are some people's times shorter? Some people may be more sensitive to the odor (have a lower odor threshold) and report the smell quicker.

- Repeat this experiment with different liquids. Smaller odor molecules diffuse more quickly. Can you tell any difference in the average diffusion times for different liquids?

- Hold the bottle about 30 cm (12 in) from your volunteer's nose and quickly squeeze the bottle so the walls are partly flattened. How quickly can you send odor molecules to someone's nose when you squeeze the bottle? How far can you send odor molecules with this method?

Experiment 2.4

Molecules through Matter—Scents and Solids

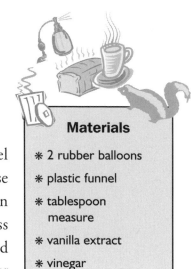

Materials

❋ 2 rubber balloons

❋ plastic funnel

❋ tablespoon measure

❋ vanilla extract

❋ vinegar

Odor molecules must travel through the air to reach your nose before you can detect a smell. Then the odor molecules must pass through your nasal passages and dissolve in the mucus covering your olfactory epithelium. Finally the molecules must reach olfactory receptors into which they can fit. However, you would not smell anything unless odor molecules could first travel through the air. Do you think odor molecules can pass through a solid the same way they pass through the air?

To begin the experiment, first smell some vinegar. Next, pour a tablespoon of vinegar through a funnel into a balloon. Do not spill any liquid on the outside of the balloon. Blow up the balloon, and tie it closed. Rinse off and dry the funnel and the tablespoon measure.

Vinegar is made of acetic acid molecules dissolved in water. When you detect the odor of vinegar, you smell acetic acid molecules. The acetic acid molecules found in vinegar have a pungent, or sharp, odor.

Smell vanilla extract. Now, pour a tablespoon of vanilla ___gh the funnel into a second balloon, and tie the ___ed.

Vanilla extract is made of vanillin molecules dissolved in an alcohol and water mixture. When you detect the odor of vanilla extract, you smell vanillin molecules. Most people recognize the smell of vanillin because it is used in many foods and is associated with vanilla flavor.

Shake each balloon for about 60 seconds. Now, smell the outside of each balloon. Do you smell vanillin on the outside of the vanilla extract balloon? Do you smell acetic acid on the outside of the vinegar balloon?

Water is a polar molecule, meaning that it has a part that is more positive and a part that is more negative (see Figure 10a). The balloon is made of rubber molecules. Rubber molecules making up the balloon do not have a more positive or negative part, so they are nonpolar molecules.

The acetic acid in vinegar is a polar molecule. It dissolves well in water but not in rubber. Vanillin is not as polar as acetic acid, so it does not dissolve as well in water. However, vanillin can dissolve in rubber better because it has a larger nonpolar part than acetic acid (see Figure 10b). Acetic acid moves through the rubber balloon more slowly than vanillin.

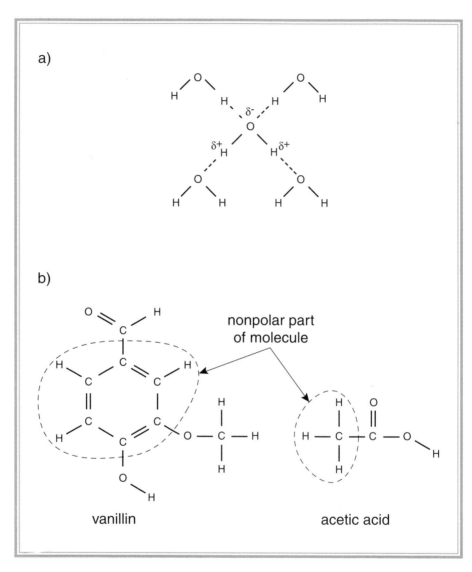

a)

b)

nonpolar part
of molecule

vanillin

acetic acid

Figure 10. a) Water molecules have a partial negative part (δ^-) and partial positive part (δ^+) and are attracted to each other through a force called hydrogen bonding. b) The vanillin molecule has a nonpolar portion that helps it dissolve in rubber better than the smaller acetic acid molecule, which tends to stay in water.

Project Ideas and Further Investigations

- Repeat the experiment using a mixture of acetic acid and vanilla extract inside the same balloon. Vanillin and acetic acid pass through rubber at different speeds and have different odor thresholds. Can you use these differences to separate one odor from the odor mixture?

  Vanillin has a lower odor threshold than acetic acid so you can detect much smaller amounts of vanillin. This difference in odor threshold makes it more complicated to say how many molecules have moved through the balloon. However, even though you can detect less vanillin, it still moves through the rubber balloon faster than acetic acid. Both its higher speed passing through the rubber and its lower odor threshold mean you will smell vanillin first on the outside of the balloon.

- Try other molecules such as peppermint extract or limonene. Limonene (a nonpolar molecule) is found in the oily liquid that can be squeezed out of an orange peel. Which odor molecules pass through a rubber balloon more quickly?

Chapter 3

Tasty Smells and Smelly Tastes

The five common senses are sight, sound, touch, smell, and taste. Smell and taste are the most closely related. One could say they are the brother and sister of the senses. Although most people do not realize it, the way food tastes has a lot to do with how it smells. Think about a time you had a cold and food lost all its appetizing taste. Did you wonder why having a cold could make food lose its taste? Most of how something tastes is really due to the way it smells. When you have a stuffy nose, odor molecules from food cannot easily get to the olfactory epithelium, and you cannot smell well. Therefore, a lot of your tasting ability is lost.

The organ used for tasting is the tongue. It is covered with tiny bumps called papillae. On every papilla there are about 200 to 300 taste buds. Taste buds are the receptors for the sense of taste. They are too tiny to see. In each taste bud there is a nerve fiber that transmits taste signals directly to the brain.

Different sections of the tongue transmit different types of taste. There are four basic tastes—sweet, sour, salty, and bitter. Recently scientists have discovered that our tongue can sense other tastes such as metallic, chalky, and umami. Umami is a Japanese word describing the meaty taste found in fish and broths. The tongue identifies the basic tastes. However, without smell, foods would have no distinct and unique character. For example, chocolate candy and strawberries are both sweet, but it is our sense of smell that gives each a different and distinct taste.

Animals have their own ways of tasting. Butterflies taste with their feet. Scallops taste with their tentacles. Catfish have taste buds covering their whole body. If you like candy, then be glad you are not a cat. They cannot taste sweetness at all.

Many animals have special tongues. For example, giraffe tongues have a built-in sunscreen. They never have to worry about getting a tongue burn. Snails have small teeth on their tongues to shred plants. Woodpeckers have sticky tongues for catching insects.

We may not have the unusual tongues of some animals, but the combination of smell and taste can still be helpful for the survival of humans. Rotten food sometimes gives off bad odors that warn us not to eat it.

As humans age, their senses tend to decline. After age 70 some people begin to lose their sense of smell. This decline in smelling ability causes food to have less taste, and can lead to a loss of appetite in some elderly people.

In this chapter you will explore the senses of taste and smell. You will discover how they work alone and together to help us sense the world around us.

Experiment 3.1

Tasting What You Smell

Materials

* onion
* potato
* apple
* knife
* an adult
* fork
* partner

We use our sense of taste every time we eat, but food would taste very different without our sense of smell. When eating, our brain can distinguish only basic tastes, such as bitter, sweet, salty, and sour. To interpret different flavors of food we depend on smell. Ninety percent of taste takes place in the olfactory epithelium, not on the tongue. In this experiment, you will discover whether people can use taste to recognize one food while they are smelling a different food.

To prepare for this experiment, cut a potato, onion, and apple in half **with adult supervision**. Next, cut a dime-sized piece off the potato, onion, and apple. Cut each piece in half. In your science notebook, set up a chart with three columns. The first column is what your partner smells, the second column is what she eats, and the third column is what she identifies as the taste.

Have your partner sit in another room, and do not let her know what foods you are using. Tell your partner to close her eyes. Then hand her a fork with a small potato piece on ⌐ partner eat the potato piece while you hold the ⌐nder her nose (see Figure 11). Do not tell your ⌐ you are holding something under her nose while

47

she chews. Ask her what she tastes, and record the answer in the chart. Then repeat this process with the second potato piece, but hold the onion half under her nose. Again, record what she says she tastes.

Do the experiment again with the apple pieces. Let your partner eat the apple pieces one at a time. Have her smell the onion the first time and the potato the second time. Finally, let your partner eat the onion pieces, first while she smells the potato and then while she smells the apple. After you have recorded your partner's answers, examine your results.

When your partner ate the potato pieces, did she identify the taste first as an apple and then as an onion? If so, this observation shows that taste is mostly determined by smell. When she smelled an apple, she may have thought she was eating an apple. When she smelled an onion, she may have thought she was eating an onion.

Figure 11. Smelling an apple while eating a small piece of potato can make you think you are eating an apple.

When your partner ate an apple or onion and smelled a potato, she may have still correctly identified the food in her mouth. If she had a potato in front of her nose, why did she still taste the apple or onion?

Have you ever laughed while drinking and had the drink come out of your nose? If so, liquid got from your mouth to your nose the same way odor molecules get from your mouth to your olfactory epithelium. The odor molecules travel in the retronasal passageway. The retronasal passageway is also known as the nasal pharynx. It is a tube going from the back of your throat to the olfactory epithelium in the nose. See Figure 12.

What happened when your partner ate an onion and smelled a potato through her nose? She probably still knew she was eating an onion. The scent molecules from the onion went up the retronasal passageway and the brain recognized the smell of onions. It also may have worked this way when your partner was eating the apple and smelling the potato.

When a person eats, odors traveling through the retronasal passageway usually dominate over odors traveling directly through the nose. Why wasn't this the case when your partner ate the

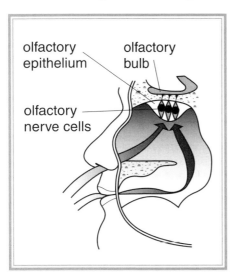

Figure 12. Odor molecules can reach the smell receptors in the olfactory epithelium through the nose or through the retronasal passageway at the back of the throat.

Project Idea and Further Investigation

You can expand this work by having volunteers smell different foods or food scents while chewing a piece of potato. Some possibilities include chocolate, peppermint, orange, vanilla extract, toast, and carrot. What kinds of food scents seem to have the most effect on taste? Apples and potatoes have a similar texture. What effect does the texture of a food have on its flavor and a person's ability to identify it? Test foods that have similar textures.

potato but smelled apple or onion? Potatoes do not have a strong smell. The olfactory epithelium received more significant odor molecules through the nose from the apple or onion than through the retronasal passageway from the potato being chewed. Your partner probably thought she was eating whatever she smelled most strongly.

You can get into a house through the front door or the back door. In somewhat the same way, molecules can get to the olfactory epithelium through the "front door" of the nose (orthonasal) or through the "back door" of the mouth and the back of the throat (retronasal).

What happened when your partner ate the apple and smelled the onion? What happened when she ate the onion and smelled the apple? How would you explain your results?

Experiment 3.2

Making Flavor Molecules

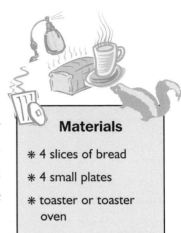

Do you prefer your bread toasted or plain? In this activity you will investigate how browning a food can change its odor and enhance the flavor.

Place one slice of plain white bread on a plate. Do not toast this slice. Toast the second piece of bread lightly and then set it on a plate. Toast the third slice of bread twice and put it on a plate. Toast the fourth slice of bread three times and then put it on a plate. The fourth slice of bread should be black on the outside. If it is not black, toast it again (see Figure 13).

Observe and record in your science notebook the color and appearance of each slice of bread. Smell each piece of bread one at a time. Try to write down an exact description of what you smell for each piece.

Can you detect a difference in smell for each piece? Does your uncooked bread have a doughy smell? Does the brown, toasted bread have a different, richer odor? Does the black bread have a still different, less desirable odor? Which piece smells the best? Which piece smells the worst?

Cooking at high temperature can cause the surface of food to turn darker. When you heat bread or meat, a chemical reaction occurs between the sugars and the amino acids in the food. Sugar units are found in carbohydrates, and amino acids are found in proteins. Amino acids are carbon compounds that link together like beads on a string to make larger protein molecules. Carbohydrates and proteins are found in both meat and bread. The reaction between amino acids and sugars produces a brown color and rich flavor. This reaction is called the Maillard reaction after the French scientist who discovered and described it.

The Maillard reaction improves taste because it creates many new molecules that add aroma and flavor to food. Roasted, broiled, and fried meats develop a brown, flavored crust, whereas boiled meats do not. Often recipes call for browning meat prior to heating it in a sauce or liquid. Browning the meat develops new flavor molecules. For a browning reaction to occur, food needs to be heated to 149–204°C (300–400°F). When the outer layer gets hot enough, the Maillard reaction occurs and the meat turns brown.

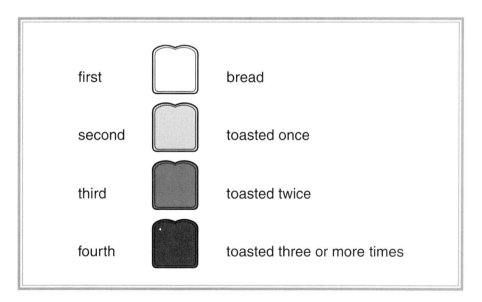

Figure 13. As you toast pieces of bread one, two, or three times how does the odor change from the original bread?

Heating molecules of sugar can make them break apart and recombine to form more than a hundred different compounds. Heating sugar to darken it is called carmelization and is sometimes used in candy making. Other examples of browning include roasting coffee and baking bread.

Project Ideas and Further Investigations

- Does the odor and flavor of a marshmallow change when you heat and brown it? Vary the temperatures and heating times of marshmallows and observe any changes in their color. **With adult supervision**, try to find the ideal heating conditions to make the best-toasted marshmallow. Place each marshmallow you test on aluminum foil on a pan and use an oven mitt to slide the tray into a hot oven.
- Sugars and amino acids are sometimes mixed and heated to create imitation flavors of meat, bread, coffee, and other foods.

  Mix together in a bowl a tablespoon of sugar and a tablespoon of flour. Place this mixture in a small aluminum foil holder, and, **with adult supervision**, heat in an oven as you did the marshmallows. After it turns brown, smell the heated mixture. Does the Maillard reaction in flour and sugar produce new odors?

Experiment 3.3

Jellybean Taste Test

Materials

* 6 resealable plastic bags (such as Ziploc bags)
* 3 flavors of jellybeans (Some jelly beans contain peanut products so if anyone doing this experiment is allergic to peanuts, check the ingredients first)
* glass of water
* 2 or more volunteers

The human brain interprets the sensation of flavor using two senses, smell and taste. Without each one the signal to the brain is not complete. In this experiment you will test the effectiveness of smell and taste working alone and together.

Separate the jellybeans into three flavors. Make sure the jellybeans are actually different flavors and not just different colors. The flavors should be listed on the package. Fill three resealable plastic bags, each with a different flavor of jellybean. Use only half of the jellybeans. These will be the taste bags. Then fill the remaining three bags, each with a different flavor. These will be the odor bags. In each odor bag, squeeze about half of the jellybeans (see Figure 14). This action will release odor molecules and make the jellybeans easier to smell.

Tell your first volunteer the three jellybean flavors you have chosen to use in this experiment. Now have y   vol-unteer close his eyes. Let him smell each odo jellybeans one at a time. After smelling each bag volunteer to identify the flavor. Instruct him not

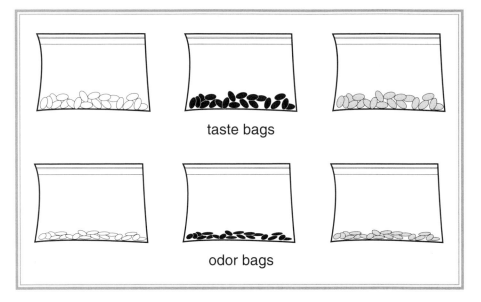

Figure 14. To compare taste and smell, make taste bags and odor bags for the three flavors of jelly beans.

he cannot recognize the flavor, he should say he doesn't know. Record how he identifies each jellybean flavor.

Have your volunteer keep his eyes closed, and now tell him to hold his nose. In no particular order, give him a jellybean from each of the taste bags. After your volunteer takes a bite of a jellybean, ask him to identify the flavor. Record his answer. After tasting each jellybean let your volunteer take a drink of water to wash the taste out of his mouth.

For the last stage of the experiment tell your volunteer to keep his eyes closed, but to let go of his nose. Once again give him each flavor of jellybean to taste one at a time. Record how he identifies each flavor. Then repeat the experiment with your second volunteer, and record her answers. Do this experiment with more people if possible.

Look at your results. Do you see any patterns? Can people identify the most flavors using their sense of smell, their sense of taste, or their senses of smell and taste together? Could some people identify flavors that others couldn't? How important was smell in determining flavor?

Everyone's taste and smell receptors are slightly different. These differences result from each person's unique body chemistry, genes, and psychology. Each person may experience the same flavor in a slightly different way. For this reason some people may have an easier time identifying flavors. Even though one smell or taste by itself may not be identifiable, together they reinforce one another, giving the complete sensation of flavor.

Project Idea and Further Investigation

Try giving your volunteer a marshmallow to eat while she is smelling a jellybean. Ask her what she tastes. Does the smell of the jellybean affect the flavor of the marshmallow? Repeat this experiment with different jellybean flavors.

Experiment 3.4

Telling Time with Your Nose

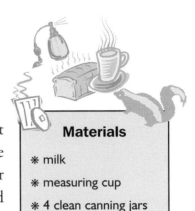

Has food ever warned you not to eat it? When food spoils, the odor of the food changes. This change in odor can serve as a warning to people and to animals not to eat the food. In this activity you will examine these odor changes. You will also find out if you can tell how long the milk has been out using only your sense of smell. You will do this experiment over a 4-day period.

The first day, pour 1/2 cup of cold milk into a clean jar and place the lid on the jar. Write the day's date and 3 DAYS OLD on a piece of masking tape, and place this tape on the jar. Set this jar in a place where it will not be disturbed and where it gets some light.

The second day, pour 1/2 cup of cold milk into a clean jar and place the lid on the jar. Write the day's date and 2 DAYS OLD on a piece of tape, and place this tape on the jar. Set this jar with the first one.

The third day, pour 1/2 cup of cold milk into a clean jar and place the lid on the jar. Write the day's date and 1 DAY OLD on a piece of tape and place this tape on the jar. Set this jar with the other two.

On the fourth day, pour 1/2 cup of cold milk into a clean jar and place a lid on the jar. Write the day's date and

FRESH on a piece of tape and place this tape on the jar (see Figure 15).

Move across the room and away from the jars. Have your partner bring each jar to you to smell. Close your eyes and have your partner briefly remove the lid while you sniff the air above each jar one at a time. Be prepared for some bad smells.

As you smell the jars of milk, identify the odors that you smell from best to worst. Identify each jar's milk odor as normal, bad, worse, or worst. You may need to smell the jars several times to place them in odor order. Open your eyes, and, with your partner's help, record how well you were able to place the jars in order from the freshest milk to the oldest milk. Switch places with your partner and let him try smelling each jar. Try to get other volunteers to smell the jars, but be sure to warn them that some of the

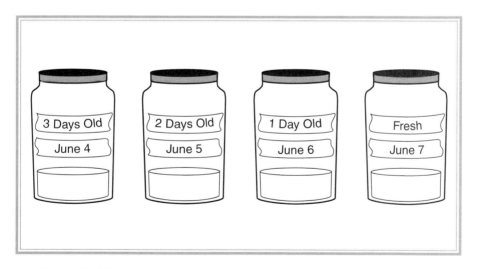

Figure 15. The smell of unrefrigerated milk changes with time as the milk spoils and "stinky" odor molecules are produced. Can you tell the age of spoiled milk?

jars of sour milk will have a bad odor. Discard the old milk and clean all the jars.

Did you find that the fresh milk you just poured into the jar smelled normal, the one-day-old milk smelled bad, the two-day-old milk smelled worse, and the three-day-old milk smelled worst? Did your nose and sense of smell tell you which milk had been out of the refrigerator the longest?

Pasteurization (developed by Louis Pasteur) is a heating process that destroys bacteria and fat-splitting enzymes in milk. Even pasteurized milk has some bacteria in it. If milk is kept cold, the bacteria will not grow much. However, if milk is kept at room temperature, the bacteria will greatly multiply. The increasing number of bacteria produce lactic acid that makes the milk turn sour. Also light shining on milk gives oxygen atoms extra energy and they react with fat molecules. This oxygen reaction breaks fat molecules into smaller odor molecules that can give spoiled milk a fishy or oily smell.

Putrid is a word that means rotten and foul-smelling. Did your milk become putrid after three days? Can you explain why the odor got worse as the milk sat out longer? Can you explain how our sense of smell can protect us from eating spoiled food?

Be sure to throw away any milk you used in these experiments. Do not drink any of this spoiled milk.

Project Idea and Further Investigation

Place 1/2 cup of milk in each of 4 different jars. Put lids on 3 of the jars. Place the first of these jars in the refrigerator. Place the second jar in a dark cabinet. Place the third jar in a sunny window. Place the fourth jar (the one with no lid) next to the third jar in the sunny window.

Notice that the conditions of the jars may be summarized as jar 1, cold, dark, closed; jar 2, warm, dark, closed; jar 3, warm, light, closed; and jar 4, warm, light, opened to fresh air. Once or twice each day for about 4 days open and smell the jars. Record the appearance of the milk and the odor of the milk in each jar. Under what conditions does the milk spoil fastest? Are you able to use what you learned in the original experiment to help explain your results?

Chapter 4

Thanks for the Memories

Have you ever heard of an electronic nose? An electronic nose has two main parts. One part is a set of sensors that respond in different ways when molecules in the air stick to them. The sensors change some property, such as color or electric resistance, to create a unique response pattern. The second part of the nose is an electronic memory that can read the response pattern. Then it identifies the pattern as a particular molecule or combination of molecules. Just like your biological olfactory system and brain, an electronic nose can remember good and bad odors.

Cyranose Science is a company that sells a walkie-talkie sized electronic nose. Their electronic nose uses thirty-two carbon sensors that swell when vapor molecules stick to them. The sensors change their resistances to create a pattern Cyranose Science calls a "smellprint."

Electronic noses have been tested for many different uses. They can detect how many days chicken has been stored or if meat is spoiled. They can tell if cooking oils have gone bad and begun to stink (gone rancid). They can tell if tomatoes were vine-ripened or picked green or even if the tomato is bruised. Doctors have experimented with diagnosing respiratory infections by using electronic noses that detect changes in breath odor. The military has developed an electronic nose that has a memory for explosives, just like bomb-sniffing dogs. The military electronic nose can detect just 1 part of explosive vapor mixed with 10 trillion (10,000,000,000,000) parts of air.

Electronic noses can remember old odors and learn new ones, just as humans do. When we smell an odor, we may not only recognize it but also remember a specific emotional feeling or memory from long ago. Some odors can instantly cause a person to have a good or bad feeling.

People learn to associate many odors with pleasant or unpleasant feelings. If a man gave a woman roses on every happy occasion in her life, how do you think she would feel when she smelled roses? If another woman only got roses from her boyfriend when they broke up, how do you think the scent of roses might make her feel? People learn to associate their memories of odors with specific events and feelings. We often have stronger emotional responses to odors than to sights or sounds.

Animals and even simple organisms must have ways to detect important odor molecules in their environment. They could not survive without their sense of smell. Smell is the most primitive sense and in humans is controlled by the limbic portion of the brain. The limbic system is the center for many basic human survival functions, including sex drive, hunger and thirst, regulation of body temperature, and emotional responses. The limbic portion of the brain includes the olfactory bulb, where odor signals are processed and remembered. People may feel an emotion from an odor before they even think about it. Smell not only helps you remember the world around you, but it also helps you feel the emotions of your past experiences. In this chapter you will investigate learning, recognizing, remembering, and describing odor memories.

Helen Keller, who was blind, deaf, and mute, learned to communicate by feeling hand symbols for letters and reading Braille, and she later learned to speak. She developed an extremely good sense of smell and strong odor memories. She could even recognize individual people from their personal odors. Helen Keller referred to the sense of smell as "a potent wizard that transports us across a thousand miles and all the years we have lived." What do you think she was telling us about odor memories?

Experiment 4.1

Molecules That Make You Remember

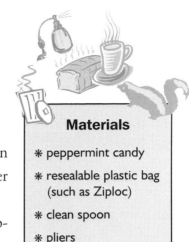

Do you think smelling a certain scent can cause people to remember something from their past?

Use the pliers to break some peppermint candy into several smaller pieces (see Figure 16). A resealable plastic bag around the pliers and the

Materials

* peppermint candy
* resealable plastic bag (such as Ziploc)
* clean spoon
* pliers
* 7 or more volunteers

candy holds the pieces when you crack it. Keep the pieces in a sealed plastic bag until you are ready to use them. Breaking the candy into pieces exposes more of the candy's surface to the air and helps release the molecules that give peppermint its distinctive scent. It is best to break the candy into pieces just before you use it so the odor is fresh and strong.

Ask your first volunteer to close her eyes. Tell your volunteer that you are going to let her smell something, and then you are going to ask her a few questions. Your volunteer should answer with the first thing that comes to her mind.

Place several pieces of the broken peppermint candy on a clean spoon. Hold the spoon below your volunteer's nose, while she keeps her eyes closed. Allow her to take several sniffs of the candy. After she has smelled the candy, ask her if the scent makes her think of a specific month of the year. Second, ask her to identify what she has smelled. Third, ask her if she had any particular thoughts or memories after she smelled the

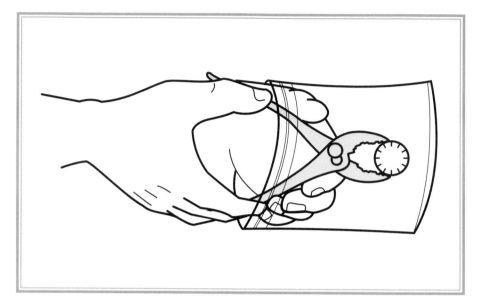

Figure 16. Use pliers to break peppermint candy into pieces. Keep the pieces in a sealed plastic bag until you are ready to test your volunteers' odor memories.

scent. Record each volunteer's answers along with his or her age and gender (male or female). Keep the peppermint pieces in a sealed bag when you are not using them.

Repeat the above procedure for each volunteer. The more people you can get to help you the better. If you are able to work with a group of several people at once, give each person a paper and pencil. Have all of your volunteers close their eyes and then expose each of them to the peppermint odor—one after the other. Next, hide the candy and ask all of them to open their eyes. Now ask them the questions given above and have them record their answers, and then write their age and gender on their paper. Collect their responses.

After you have collected information from as many different people as you can—one at a time or in small groups, you can analyze the results. Consider the following questions. How many people (by number and percent of the total) identified the scent as peppermint? How many people identified the month as December? How many of the people that identified the month as December also recognized the odor as peppermint? How many of the people that did not identify the month as December recognized the odor as peppermint? How many of your volunteers had specific memories triggered by the peppermint scent, and what were those memories?

Odor signals from the olfactory bulb are first analyzed in the limbic system (the portion of our brains where emotions are processed) before signals are sent to the cerebrum (a higher portion of our brains where reasoning takes place). Because of this process, we may feel an emotion from an odor before we even think about what the odor is.

In our minds, unique odors are often strongly connected with specific memories. When we recognize an odor, our brains automatically search our memory-odor connection to determine if that odor goes with a good or bad experience.

A person who was a soldier in a war may associate a burning smell with gunfire and battles. However, a child may associate the same burning smell with birthday candles. Thus, the same odor could trigger bad feelings and unpleasant memories in one person and good feelings and happy memories in another person. Through our experiences, we learn to link certain odors with specific memories.

In this activity, we selected peppermint because this candy has a distinctive scent that most people can recognize, and because it is much more common during the December holiday season.

Project Idea and Further Investigation

Try using other scents that might trigger strong memories in a variety of people. Some possibilities include the aroma of roasted turkey, the smell of cut grass, spices used in cooking, hot pizza, or the smell of Play-Doh. For this activity, simply expose different people to a distinctive odor while their eyes are closed, and then ask them what thoughts or memories they have.

Experiment 4.2

Learning New Smells

You learn new information all the time. For example, you study spelling words or science facts to prepare for tests. Do you think you could learn to recognize new odors the same way you learn how to spell new words? In this activity you will work with several volunteers to see if they can learn new smells.

Materials

∗ almond extract

∗ banana extract

∗ orange extract

∗ peppermint extract

∗ vanilla extract
(These flavoring extracts are sold in grocery stores. The banana extract may be labeled imitation.)

∗ 3 or more young volunteers (not adults)

Have your first volunteer sit at a table facing you. Ask her to close her eyes. Arrange the 5 bottles of flavor extract (almond, banana, orange, peppermint, and vanilla) on the table in front of you. Open one of the bottles and hold it an inch or two beneath her nose. Ask her to identify the smell and record her answer. Figure 17 shows one way to record the data you collect for each volunteer. Close that bottle and open the next one. Have her smell the second bottle and record her answer. Repeat this procedure for all 5 bottles—almond, banana, orange, peppermint, and vanilla.

Now look at the results that you have recorded from the testing. Identify which odors your volunteer did not get correct. Let her smell each odor that she missed, but this time tell her the name of the odor. After you have repeated this

Science Fair Success with Scents, Aromas, and Smells

Learning New Smells—Experiment Results
Volunteer: Joe Smith, Age 14

Date/Test #	Almond	Banana	Orange	Peppermint	Vanilla
Jan 23					
Test 1	strawberry	not sure	orange	peppermint	not sure
	TRAIN	*TRAIN*			*TRAIN*
Test 2	not sure	banana	almond	peppermint	vanilla
	TRAIN		*TRAIN*		
Test 3	almond	banana	orange	peppermint	vanilla
Jan 24					
Test 1	orange	banana	almond	peppermint	vanilla
	TRAIN		*TRAIN*		
Test 2	almond	banana	orange	peppermint	vanilla
Jan 25					
Test 1	. . .	. . .	. . .	. . .	. . .

Figure 17. Prepare a chart for each volunteer with a record of their responses before and after you have trained them to identify scents. The correct odor is listed across the top and the person's responses are shown for each date and test.

training procedure for each of the missed odors, repeat the original testing.

One at a time, open the 5 bottles and hold each beneath her nose. Ask her to identify each smell and record her answer. Do not present the odors in the same order as you did in the first testing experiment. Each time you test a volunteer, present the odors in a different order. You do not want your volunteers to anticipate what odor will come next.

The next day repeat the testing and training procedure. Test and train every day, until your volunteer can correctly identify all 5 smells the first time she smells them.

Wait about a week and test your volunteer again. Wait several more weeks and test her again.

Work with your other volunteers the same way. Test and train each day until they can correctly identify all the odors on the first test of that day. Each time you test, change the order in which you present the odors.

Were your volunteers able to learn new odors? Did they remember the new odors a week or several weeks later?

Most young people will not recognize all the odors the first time they are tested. They may recognize only a few fragrant food extracts. Which odors were the easiest for your volunteers to recognize? Which were the most difficult to recognize? How would you explain this difference?

As people are repeatedly trained and tested, they should come to know all 5 flavoring odors. What did your results show? Could your volunteers correctly identify the odors when they were tested several weeks later? Once an odor is truly learned, it may be like riding a bike—something you never forget.

Project Idea and Further Investigation

You can continue this investigation using several adult volunteers. Are the adults able to identify more or fewer odors on the first test than your younger volunteers? Are the adults able to learn more or less rapidly than young people? You can also try different sources of smells such as bay leaves, ginger, cinnamon, or cloves.

Research indicates that within two days of birth a newborn baby can use his sense of smell to recognize his mother. An adult's sense of smell is usually best between 20 to 40 years of age. However, a person's sense of smell may decline greatly after age 70. Does your investigation lead you to any observations about how age affects the learning of new odors?

Experiment 4.3

Recognizing Rotting Fruit

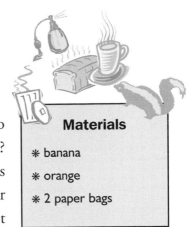

How do you think you learn to recognize the smell of rotten fruit? Do you have a memory of what is rotten based on its smell from earlier experiences? Or did you just instinctively know the smell of

rotting fruit the first time you encountered it? Although scientists are not sure of the answers to these questions, they know that humans associate certain odors with certain situations. Both sight and smell can warn us not to eat a food that might make us sick.

Some poisonous tree frogs contain chemicals that will make an animal sick if it eats the frog. An animal that gets sick will not eat that type of frog again. Predator animals learn to avoid frogs with the same unique color markings.

In this experiment you will keep a daily smell journal. You will try to determine how long it takes for two types of fruit to go bad. Does it take days, weeks, or months for the fruit to rot if left out in the room? Place an orange and a banana in two paper bags and put them where they can be left for many days without being disturbed. Each day, record the date and then describe the color, appearance, and odor of each piece of fruit in your smell journal. Describe whether the appearance or odor seems different from the day before. Write down any changes you observe.

Fruits and vegetables rot because microbes, such as mold, grow on them at higher temperatures. Fruits also rot because they have special chemicals called enzymes that break apart molecules. If you drop a fruit and bruise it, cell walls are broken and these enzymes are released. The fruit will then turn brown or black where it is damaged.

After many days can you see mold growing on your fruit? Do the smells of the orange and banana change with time? How long does it take for each fruit to rot?

Have you ever seen mold growing on bread? How did the bread smell?

Be sure to throw away any food you use in these experiments. Do not eat any of this spoiled fruit.

Project Ideas and Further Investigations

- For this investigation you will need three fresh bananas, a yardstick, and three paper bags. The bananas need to be about the same size, with no bruises or dark spots. Label the three paper bags as NOT DROPPED, DROPPED 1 YARD, and DROPPED 2 YARDS. Place the first banana in the bag marked NOT DROPPED. Drop the second banana from a height of 1 yard onto a hard floor. Place the second banana in the bag marked DROPPED 1 YARD. Drop the third banana from a height of 2 yards onto a hard floor. Place the third banana in the bag marked DROPPED 2 YARDS.

  Check the appearance, color, and odor of each banana after 1 hour, 2 hours, 3 hours, 1 day, and then once each day until you stop. Keep a smell journal and record your observations. How did dropping the fruit affect the rotting process? Since temperature can affect the rate of rotting, all the fruit needs to be kept in the same place, at the same temperature. Record the temperature. Can you think of an experiment to test the effect of temperature on rotting?

Experiment 4.4

Describing Odors

Can people describe what they smell as well as they can describe what they see?

For this experiment you need volunteers who have seen and smelled a rose. Ask your first volunteer to think of the appearance and the smell of a rose. Tell your volunteer to imagine a particular rose. Now ask him to describe, without using the words "flower" or "rose," the exact appearance of this rose. He can imagine describing the rose to a person who has never before seen one. Ask your volunteer to write down his description.

Now ask him to think carefully about how this rose smells. Ask him to write down, without using the words "flower" or "rose," an exact description of the scent of this rose.

Repeat this procedure for other volunteers, or you can have several people write their answers at once. Remember, you are not telling any of your volunteers what to write—that is left entirely to them. If you can get more people to take part in this activity, it will make a better survey.

How does our vocabulary for describing smells compare to our vocabulary for describing sights? Could your volunteers describe the appearance of a rose? Did your volunteers have trouble thinking of words to describe the fragrance of the rose? Did you find any of your volunteers saying "A rose smells like a rose" or "I can't think of what to write"? Compare the visual descriptions with the odor descriptions. How many words were used in each type of description? Were the visual or odor description more detailed?

When people describe something they see, they have a rich vocabulary to use. Because humans often think and talk about what they see, they can describe the size, shape, color, and texture of an object. People can remember what they have seen in a way that they cannot recall odors. When you think of a rose, you instantly see it in your mind. However, do you smell it in your mind?

People can tell the difference between many odors. However, if asked to describe an odor, most people usually refer to something else that has a similar odor. People might say "It smells like a rose" or "It smells like chocolate", but cannot otherwise describe it.

Some people who work in the perfume industry have trained themselves to identify hundreds or even thousands of different scents, and they have a much richer vocabulary to deal with smells than most people. Maybe if you try to concentrate on what you smell, you can think of words that fit the odors of your world.

Project Ideas and Further Investigations

- As a follow-up to Experiment 4.4, you can take the written descriptions and show them to two groups of volunteers—one to read the visual descriptions and one to read the scent descriptions. How many people from the first group can identify the rose from the visual description? How many people from the second group can identify the rose from the odor description?

- You can repeat this activity with other objects, such as chocolate, that have an interesting smell and appearance. Hand each volunteer a piece of chocolate. Ask her to look at the chocolate and to smell it. Tell your volunteer to carefully describe the appearance of the chocolate and the odor of the chocolate without using the words "candy" or "chocolate." Compare the results as you did for the rose study.

- There are flavor wheels that use standard words to help give people a vocabulary to describe odors. A flavor wheel still uses specific items to represent odors, but helps give people working in food, wine, and perfume industries a language to describe odors. You can read more about flavor wheels or order a color copy of one from the first Internet site listed in the back of the book.

Chapter 5

Agreeable Aromas and Sensational Scents

Aromas and scents are all around us. People may use a certain soap, shampoo, cologne, or perfume because of its smell. We may decide whether to try a new kind of food by how appealing it smells. We use our sense of smell all the time, but we don't depend on smelling for our daily survival. However, animals must constantly use their sense of smell for survival. In the animal world, odors are used to communicate, locate food, find mates, and avoid danger.

Certain fragrances can alter feelings and bring pleasure to humans. When odor molecules enter a person's nose and reach the olfactory epithelium, they are converted into electrical nerve signals. These signals are transmitted to the olfactory bulb. The fragrance signals are then processed in the limbic system of the brain. Since the limbic system controls our emotions, smells can trigger good and bad feelings.

Every year companies spend millions of dollars producing new perfumes and colognes that consumers will want to buy. These companies make up the large and successful fragrance industry. Chemists, perfumers, sales people, marketing experts, managers, and even psychologists play important roles in this industry.

Perfumes were originally made of natural products obtained from flowers, animals, wood products, and so forth. Today, more synthetically produced ingredients are being used in perfumes. Specially trained chemists are able to reproduce natural scents, and also come up with new ones.

Perfumers train their olfactory memories so they are able to remember thousands of scents and blends of scents. They are responsible for first imagining, then preparing the complicated mixtures that make up new perfumes and colognes. Psychologists play an important role in the fragrance industry by conducting experiments on the effects of scents and fragrances on human emotion and performance.

Sensational scents and fabulous fragrances are all around us. We use perfumes, colognes, and essential plant oils for various reasons. We may simply enjoy the smell. The fragrance may produce certain emotions that we enjoy, or it may bring back pleasant memories. Some odors may be used for relaxation and others for mental alertness. Whatever the reason, humans are so attracted to agreeable aromas that they are willing to spend lots of money on fragrances captured in bottles. Very detailed research goes along with finding the right scent to attract consumers. In this chapter you will learn some of the scientific aspects of these agreeable aromas, fabulous fragrances, and sensational scents.

Experiment 5.1

Perfume on Different Surfaces

Materials

* bottle of perfume with a spray nozzle
* spoon
* paper
* cotton rag
* clock or watch

The first perfumes used were in the form of incense. They were burned to show respect for the gods in ancient cultures. Today, the most popular type of perfume is bought as a liquid in a bottle. These bottles of perfumes or colognes are called fragrances. The definition of a fragrance is a mix of oils in a 75 percent to 95 percent alcohol solution.

The different ingredients used in fragrances have different "notes." There are three notes in a fragrance—the top, middle, and bottom notes. These are not notes you hear, but notes you smell. The top note is the first scent to evaporate when a perfume is applied. Top notes are usually flower oils. The middle note takes about ten minutes to begin evaporating from the skin. Middle notes are the body of the fragrance, and they are classified into such groups as floral, chypre, green, spicy, or oriental. The bottom note is the lingering scent of the fragrance. Bottom notes are animal or wood products.

We smell different notes of the fragrance as it evaporates from our skin. Will the rate and amount of the perfume that evaporates change on different materials? Let's find out in this experiment.

Before you begin the experiment, make a chart in your science notebook, listing along the top of the page the objects that will be sprayed with perfume: spoon, cloth, paper, and wrist. On the left side, going down the page, list the time in minutes: 0, 15, 30, 45, 60. These times are how long the perfume has been on the object.

Lay out the spoon, cotton rag, and piece of paper. Then apply the same amount of perfume to each object and to your wrist. When applying the perfume, spray each object once from about 13 cm (5 in) away. Make sure to remember the specific place you sprayed the perfume.

Smell each object. Record how strong the perfume smells on each object. In your chart give each object a number, 1 through 4. Label the object with the strongest scent NUMBER 1. Label the object with the second strongest scent

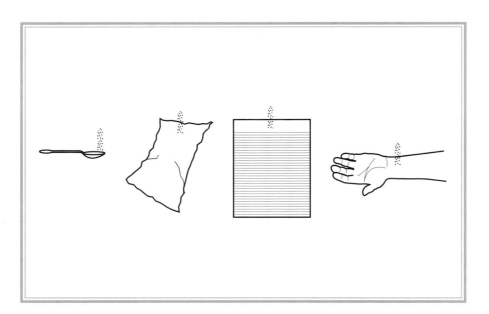

Figure 18. Compare the smell of perfume from a spoon, a cotton rag, a piece of paper, and a person's wrist. The scents from each can vary with time and vary from each other.

NUMBER 2, and so on. Record this information every 15 minutes for 60 minutes.

As you smell the objects (see Figure 18), try observing different qualities of the perfume. Record any significant changes you observe. Does the perfume smell different on each object? Is it stronger on some objects and weaker on others?

After the 60 minutes is up, look at your chart. Do the oils in perfume evaporate more quickly from paper, cloth, metal, or your skin? The more oil that is evaporating, the stronger the object will smell. Do some objects start off smelling strong and then weaken? Can you tell if the top, middle, and bottom notes are evaporating at different rates? Can you think of ways to describe how the odor changes with time?

Project Ideas and Further Investigations

- Try the same experiment with different objects. Use the data from the previous experiment to predict which materials will have the strongest smell.

  - Try leaving the perfume on for longer amounts of time. For example leave it on for 6 hours and smell the objects every hour. Does this change your results? Why or why not?

Experiment 5.2

Making Your Own Perfume

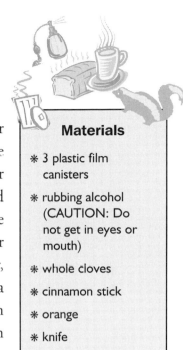

Perfume has been used for thousands of years. Long before department stores and designer fragrances existed, people around the world used perfume. The Assyrians put perfume on their beards. Nero, a Roman emperor, took baths in rose wine. Cleopatra had the sails of her barge soaked in perfume to receive the Roman general Mark Antony. The French emperor Napoleon used a bottle or two of perfume every day.

Materials

* 3 plastic film canisters

* rubbing alcohol (CAUTION: Do not get in eyes or mouth)

* whole cloves

* cinnamon stick

* orange

* knife

One reason many people used large amounts of perfume in the past was because they did not bathe very often. Today people do not perfume beards or boats, but producing perfume is a major industry. It costs more than 20 million dollars for a new scent of perfume to be produced. Last year the worldwide sales of fragrances totaled more than 15 billion dollars. With such a high demand for new scents, people in the perfume business are developing new scents faster. Twenty years ago it took one to three years to develop a new scent. Now, some new scents are developed in a few months.

In this experiment you will make three simplified versions of perfumes. The perfumes in this experiment only have two ingredients. (Most commercial perfumes contain anywhere from 10 to 500 ingredients.)

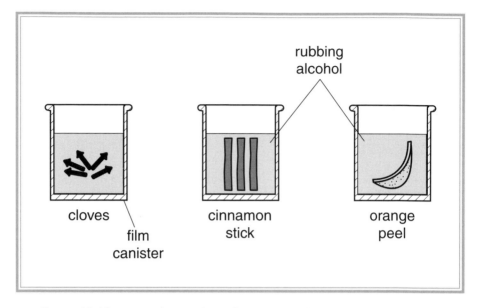

Figure 19. You can make simple perfumes with rubbing alcohol and cloves, cinnamon, or orange peel.

To make your perfume, fill three plastic film canisters about halfway with rubbing alcohol. In the first canister, add 5 cloves to the alcohol. Now break the cinnamon stick into about 5 pieces. Add 3 of those pieces to the second canister. Cut an orange into 8 slices. Take the peel off one orange slice and tear the peel in half. Roll up that half and place it in the third canister of rubbing alcohol (see Figure 19).

Put the tops on all 3 canisters. Let your perfume mixtures sit for 3 days. On the third day, your perfume should be ready. Use your finger to rub the alcohol from each canister on your wrist. At first you may just smell rubbing alcohol, but as it evaporates the scent of citrus or spices should come through.

Commercial perfumes have additional ingredients. Almost all store-bought perfumes include natural oils, aroma chemicals, fixatives, and alcohol. The alcohol that you used in your perfume dissolved the chemicals in the ingredients you added. It acted as a carrier of the fragrance.

You may notice that your perfume fragrance does not last very long. Fixatives are used to make the smell of perfume last. The lack of a fixative in your perfume may be why the scent did not linger. Fixatives slow the evaporation rate so that the perfume will not all evaporate in the first few minutes. Fixatives are chemicals that come from natural mosses or resins, or they are made in a lab.

Perfumes used to have only natural ingredients, like those used in the perfumes you made. Today aroma chemicals are also used in perfume. These chemicals are produced in labs. They may copy the smells of nature, or they may be unique odors developed by a chemist.

Project Ideas and Further Investigations

- Get creative! Mix and match ingredients. Try developing your own original perfume. Mix ingredients used in Experiment 5.2 or think of your own ingredients. For example, you could try to combine cinnamon, orange peel, and vanilla all in one canister.
- Make perfumes with more or less alcohol than used in Experiment 5.2. Does the amount of alcohol affect the strength of your perfume's odor?

Experiment 5.3

Food Odors and Mood

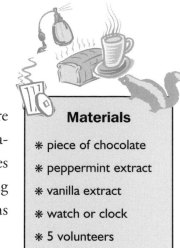

The limbic system, where odors are processed, includes the hypothalamus. The hypothalamus regulates many bodily functions, including emotions, so smells and emotions are closely related.

Materials

* piece of chocolate
* peppermint extract
* vanilla extract
* watch or clock
* 5 volunteers

Aromatherapy is a form of therapy that claims smells affect a person's emotions and state of mind. Aromatherapists use essential oils to produce certain emotions. Essential oils are natural oils extracted from the leaves, fruits, flowers, roots, or seeds of a variety of plants. These oils may be sprayed, inhaled, or used in a massage. Some people think essential oils initiate feelings such as relaxation or alertness.

A new study of the relationship between odors and moods is called Aroma-Chology. It was developed in 1989 by the Olfactory Research Fund (now known as the Sense of Smell Institute). Aroma-Chology uses scientific methods to determine the psychological effects of the odors used in aromatherapy. Aroma-Chology also involves the research of blends of odors, such as those used in perfumes.

This activity will allow you to explore how different food odors influence a person's mood. You need at least 5 volunteers for this activity, but more people would give a better sampling.

Before starting this activity, make a chart in your science notebook to record your observations. Along the top of the chart, list the 3 materials: vanilla, peppermint, and chocolate. On the left side of the chart going down the page, write your helpers' names or number them as volunteer 1, 2, 3, etc.

You will perform this experiment with each volunteer, one at a time. Have your first volunteer sit in a quiet room with his eyes closed so he can concentrate on what he smells without distractions. Tell your volunteer you are going to let him smell peppermint, vanilla, or chocolate and then ask him a question about how he feels.

Open the bottle of vanilla extract and hold it about 5 cm (2 in) beneath your volunteer's nose. Hold it there for about a minute. Then close the bottle and ask him if he feels more or less hungry, more or less relaxed, more or less energetic, or no different than before he smelled the food odor. Ask your volunteer to pick one of these 7 choices.

Repeat this process with a bottle of peppermint extract and a piece of chocolate. Wait at least a minute between each odor you give your volunteer to smell. Record all the volunteers' responses (see Figure 20).

Look at the results in your chart. Did the odors have any effect on the volunteers' reported moods? Did the odors affect people in similar ways, or were the reactions different?

When people smell foods they enjoy, it can cause them to develop an appetite. This can produce good feelings. How did people react to the food you had them smell? Did anyone say it made him hungry? Some researchers have claimed to use odors to reduce appetite and help people lose weight. Smelling a food or other odor for long enough may make you feel full

Sample Food Odors and Mood

Volunteer #	Vanilla	Peppermint	Chocolate
1	MORE RELAXED	MORE HUNGRY	LESS HUNGRY
2	MORE RELAXED	MORE ENERGETIC	MORE HUNGRY
3	NO DIFFERENT	MORE ENERGETIC	MORE HUNGRY

Figure 20. Make a chart to show if your volunteers report any change in mood when they smell vanilla, peppermint, or chocolate.

even if you have not eaten anything. Have you ever heard someone who has been cooking or working in a restaurant say they do not feel hungry because they have been smelling food?

Vanilla and peppermint are both essential oils used in aromatherapy. Aromatherapists use vanilla to produce relaxation and reduce stress. They use peppermint to lift moods and stimulate the brain. In your experiment, did these oils have any measurable effect?

In Japan the effect of peppermint on moods has been tested in nursing homes, hospitals, and factories. These tests found that the odor of peppermint increased alertness and decreased boredom. In another study, peppermint odors were found to increase brain waves associated with alertness.

Did chocolate cause people to become hungry or did smelling it reduce their hunger?

Project Idea and Further Investigation

Try the original experiment but have your volunteer close her eyes and just smell air. Do not tell her that there is no bottle under her nose, but tell her the odor will be extremely faint or hard to detect. Sometimes people report a change or experience a benefit in medicine even when no medicine is given. This type of change, when nothing is actually done, is called the placebo effect. Do any of your volunteers report a change or placebo effect from odorless air? How do you think the placebo effect complicates medical research?

Experiment 5.4

Essential Oils and Attracting Insects

Essential oils are the part of plants that give them their unique smell. Essential oils can be found in almost

Materials

* banana

every part of a plant. They are found in flowers, grass, stems, seeds, leaves, bark, and fruits. Plants containing essential oils are important to the perfume industry. These types of plants have been present on the earth for millions of years. Fossils of roses have been found that are 20 million to 30 million years old.

Essential oils are the basic ingredients for perfumes. Although many fragrances are synthetically produced instead of extracted from plants, some perfume makers are going back to using only natural essential oils in their perfumes.

There are many methods used to extract an essential oil from a plant. These methods include expression, distillation, maceration, enfleurage, and extraction. Expression is used to get oils from citrus fruits. In expression, the fruit's peel is pressed until it secretes the liquid oil. Distillation is a way of getting oils from flowers, seeds, and leaves. Flowers or other plant parts are placed in boiling water and the essential oil is carried in the steam, which is caught in droplets. In maceration, flowers are put in hot fats and then washed with alcohol. Enfleurage is similar to maceration, except that cold fats are used instead of hot ones. Extraction is the most common method of obtaining essential oils. It is used for petals, leaves, and roots. In extraction, plants are placed with a solvent chemical into a sealed container. The solvent dissolves the essential oil.

Humans use essential oils to help make perfumes smell good. However, animals are attracted to the smell of essential oils because they know the plant can be a source of food. In this experiment you will discover if the odor of a banana can attract insects.

Insects have incredible smelling capabilities. Humans receive most of their information from sight, but insects depend mostly on smell and taste to get information about the world around them. Insects smell with their antennae. The antennae are covered with odor receptors. Insects communicate with each other by giving off scents that have special messages. When an ant finds food it lets the other ants in its colony know by leaving a scent trail to the food, and passing the scent message to other ants with its antennae.

Peel a banana and place it outside on the ground. Wait a day, then check on the banana. Has it attracted any insects? What types? How many insects are on or around the banana? Check the banana each day for several days. How long does it take for insects to sense the odor of the essential oils in the banana and come to it as a source of food?

Project Ideas and Further Investigations

- Try to discover which fruits' essential oils attract the most insects and the greatest variety of insects. Place a peeled banana, an apple half, and an orange half outside. Make sure they are at least 3 m (10 ft) apart. Wait a day, then observe each piece of fruit. Record the types of insects and the number of insects on or around each fruit. Check the fruit each day for several days, and record any changes in the fruits' appearance, any odor you smell, and the number and type of insects present.

- Buy bottles of banana extract and orange extract at a grocery store. Place two pieces of notebook paper about 3 m (10 ft) apart on the ground outside and use rocks or other weights to hold them down. Pour about 30 mL (6 teaspoons) of banana oil on one paper and the same amount of orange oil on the other paper. Check the papers each day for several days. Were you able to attract any insects with just the essential oil but no fruit?

Chapter 6

Stop the Stink

If you are in a room with a constant bad odor, eventually you may not even notice it. However, someone who just enters the room will immediately smell the bad odor. The sense of smell responds best to either a new or stronger odor. An odor is strongest when you first smell it. In our daily life there are many mildly unpleasant odors or extremely bad odors (malodors) that have a strong stench. People use a variety of ways to try to reduce or eliminate bad odors.

Teenagers and adults can use deodorants and antiperspirants to control the body odor that comes from armpits. The armpit provides a moist, warm environment for bacteria to grow. Antiperspirants keep the armpit drier and thus reduce bacterial growth. Deodorants destroy or counteract the odors or reduce bacterial growth. Bacteria turn the organic compounds in sweat into smelly compounds. A particular person's body odor comes from the combination of dozens of volatile compounds. However, in 1990, scientists at the Monell Chemical Senses Center in Philadelphia found that one of the main smells of body odor is due to a particular molecule called 3-methyl-2-hexenoic acid, or $C_6H_{12}O_2$.

There are many sources of malodors, including sewage, animal wastes, animal odors, decaying meat, rotting fruit, bacteria, molds, and industrial chemicals. Once a malodor is in the air, there are several ways to try to control it. These methods include adsorption, oxidation, neutralization, masking, and counteraction.

When molecules stick to the surface of carbon powder, it is called adsorption. Odor molecules can be removed from air by adsorption. In 1993, New York City was using forty-four large towers to help adsorb gases vented from their sewage-treatment system. Each tower held 10,000 kilograms (22,000 pounds) of carbon powder.

Oxidation is a chemical process that can change the stinky molecule to a different form by exposing it to oxygen. Machines that produce ozone (O_3) are sometimes used to oxidize smelly molecules.

Neutralization is a chemical reaction whereby an acid and a base react to one another. Hydrogen sulfide is an acidic molecule given off by decomposing sewage or in the production of paper. Strong bases, such as sodium hydroxide, can neutralize hydrogen sulfide.

Introducing a new, pleasant odor that is stronger than the old, unpleasant odor is called masking. You may only be able to detect or smell the stronger of the two odors even though the bad one is still there. Most room deodorizers work by masking.

Counteraction (also called vector addition masking) uses pairs of odors that tend to cancel each other out. Either a milder pleasant odor is produced or neither odor is smelled. These special pairs are called Zwaardemaker pairs after the Dutch scientist who discovered them. Guy Paschal worked to find pleasant odors that would compete with offensive odors. The first widespread commercial application of this method was the deodorizing product known as Airwick. Airwick was introduced in the 1940s by William H. Wheeler. Wheeler was the founder and president of Airkem Inc. By 1959, Airkem and Airwick products were sold in more than a hundred countries.

In this chapter you will explore some of the ways that people stop stinky smells.

Experiment 6.1

Neutralizing Odors

Perhaps you have seen someone put
an opened box of baking soda in a
refrigerator to help eliminate bad
odors. In this experiment, you will
investigate how baking soda can
absorb molecules from the air and
neutralize acids.

Add 2 tablespoons of vinegar to
the bottom of each of 2 plastic bowls.
Cut off the top of a plastic cup so it
is about 5 cm (2 in) high. Place 3
tablespoons of baking soda into the

Materials
* 2 large plastic bowls with tight-sealing lids
* 2 tablespoons
* disposable plastic cup
* scissors
* vinegar
* baking soda

cup, then place this cup into one of the plastic bowls. Sniff the
air above each bowl. Tightly seal the lid of each bowl. Set
the sealed bowls in a place where they can remain undisturbed
for several weeks (see Figure 21).

Wait one week and then remove the lid from the baking
soda and vinegar bowl. Sniff the air just above the bowl.
Replace the lid. Remove the lid from the vinegar bowl, and
sniff the air just above the bowl. Replace the lid.

Wait another week and repeat this sniffing procedure. Wait
a third week and repeat this sniffing procedure for the last
time.

Each time you smell the pair of bowls, record which one
has a stronger vinegar odor. Observe which one seems to have
more vinegar liquid in it.

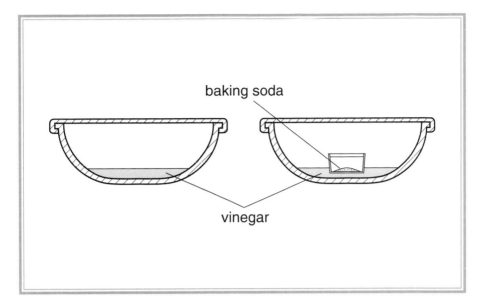

Figure 21. Baking soda in a cup can absorb moisture and odor molecules from the air inside a closed plastic bowl.

After three weeks, which bowl had the weaker vinegar smell? Which bowl had less vinegar in it?

Vinegar is a mixture of mostly water and about 5 percent acetic acid ($C_2H_4O_2$). The acetic acid gives vinegar a strong, pungent odor. Baking soda (sodium bicarbonate, or $NaHCO_3$) is a base. When an acid and a base are combined, they can neutralize each other. Fruits and many other foods contain acids. Baking soda in a refrigerator can help neutralize these acid odor molecules.

After three weeks, was most of the liquid vinegar gone from the bowl containing the baking soda? Where do you think it went?

If you could weigh the baking soda, you would find that it weighs more after three weeks in the bowl. The solid baking soda absorbs water and acetic acid molecules from the air. As more molecules go from the liquid into the air, they continue to be trapped by the baking soda. Gradually more and more molecules become trapped in the baking soda. Do you see why baking soda is effective in removing both bad odors and excess moisture from a refrigerator?

Project Ideas and Further Investigations

- Repeat this experiment with pure water or other liquids, like soft drinks. Does the type of liquid cause a difference in how quickly it is absorbed? Repeat this experiment with larger amounts of baking soda. Does using more baking soda absorb the liquids more rapidly?

- Try other solids, such as uncooked rice, salt, and sugar, and see if these solids can absorb water from the air. Can they also remove odor molecules from the air?

Experiment 6.2

Smelly Feet and Carbon that Grabs Molecules

Materials

* 2 stinky socks
* 2 resealable plastic bags (such as Ziploc bags)
* package of Odor-Eaters or other foot-odor-control insoles
* volunteer with stinky feet
* scissors

Do you have any friends or family members who tend to have stinky feet? If so, that is good. You need their help. You need a volunteer to wear a pair of socks all day and then give you his smelly socks for this experiment. It is best if he has exercised or gotten hot so his socks are moist and smelly.

Smell each sock and describe what you smell in your science notebook. Place one moist, smelly sock in a resealable plastic bag and seal it. Cut an Odor-Eater insole into about six pieces. (Odor-Eaters are sold in grocery stores and pharmacies and are used inside shoes to help control foot odor.) Place all six pieces in the second resealable plastic bag. Add the other moist, smelly sock to this bag and seal it.

The next day, open the first bag and sniff. Then open the second bag, remove the Odor-Eater pieces, and sniff the bag. Return the Odor-Eater pieces to the bag and reseal both bags. Record your smell observations. Repeat this activity each day for three days. Compare the smell of the bags with ~~~ ~ ~ out the Odor-Eaters.

Odor-Eaters contain baking soda and act Baking soda neutralizes acid odor molecul

moisture and odor molecules. Activated charcoal is a carbon powder that has a rough surface with many small pores. The pores in this rough surface provide many places where odor molecules can stick. If the odor molecules are stuck on the carbon powder, then you will not be able to smell them because they cannot reach your nose.

Feet sweat and produce moisture, which becomes trapped in socks. Feet also stay warm inside enclosed shoes. This moisture and warmth create a perfect environment for bacteria and fungi to grow. You have some bacteria all over your body, but when you give the bacteria and fungi a warm, moist place they can grow more rapidly and produce unpleasant aromas. You may smell ammonia or something that smells like old butter when you smell stinky socks. Bacteria and fungi on your feet produce these odor molecules. If you do not want stinky feet, keep them clean and dry.

Project Idea and Further Investigation

See if you can develop experiments to answer any of the following questions: Do older or younger people tend to have smellier feet? How does the smell of a sock relate to a person's amount of exercise? How does wetness of socks affect their odor? Can you develop a stink scale with numbers to judge how bad socks or shoes smell?

Experiment 6.3

Room Deodorizers and Masking

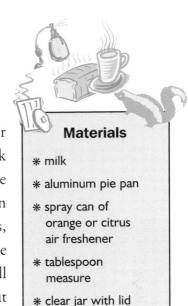

People often have odors in their homes, schools, or places of work that they don't want. These unpleasant odors may be found in bathrooms, closets, diaper pails, trash cans, cars, or a pet's bed. One way to eliminate an unpleasant smell is to cover it with a stronger, but more pleasant, smell. This method of covering up an odor is called masking.

Materials

* milk
* aluminum pie pan
* spray can of orange or citrus air freshener
* tablespoon measure
* clear jar with lid
* measuring cup

There are many different types of air fresheners (also called room deodorizers) sold in stores. These devices include sprays, scented candles, liquids or solids that evaporate at room temperature, and devices that plug into a wall to heat a liquid or solid and put vapor into the air. In this experiment, you will test how well an air freshener can mask a bad odor.

Place 1/2 cup of fresh milk in a clear jar. Place a lid on the jar, and let it sit out in a room for three days.

After three days, open the jar and stir the spoiled milk. Place 2 tablespoons of the spoiled milk in the aluminum pie pan. Smell the pie pan. How does it smell? Spray citrus or orange air freshener on the pie pan (see Figure 22). Smell the pie pan again. Repeat the spraying and smelling several times until you cannot smell the spoiled milk.

Figure 22. Can a room deodorizer mask the smell of spoiled milk?

Let the pie pan sit overnight and then smell it. How does it smell?

Both good and bad odors are detected by a person's olfactory receptors. However, if there is enough of the pleasant odor, only that odor is recognized. By adding enough of the good odor, the bad odor is no longer recognized by the brain, even though it is still present.

Spoiled milk has an extremely unpleasant odor. Did the spoiled milk smell bad? How many times did you have to spray it with air freshener before you could only smell a pleasant orange or citrus odor? Fragrant oils from orange and other citrus peels contain pleasant-smelling compounds that are often used in air fresheners.

As the pleasant odor gradually fades, the bad odor that was masked may come back. After you waited overnight, did the sour milk odor return or did the citrus odor remain?

Project Ideas and Further Investigations

• Try repeating this experiment but use a variety of different air fresheners. Compare these room deodorizers to determine which one acts fastest, which one is strongest, and which one lasts the longest.

• Try sprinkling baking soda on the spoiled milk to neutralize the odor (see Experiment 6.1). Try different amounts of baking soda and compare the results after different amounts of time.

Experiment 6.4

Something Smells Fishy

Some people squeeze lemon juice on fish or other seafood before they eat it. In this investigation, you will explore the connection between lemon juice, fish, and fishy odors.

Pour 1/2 cup of water into a bowl. Add 1/2 cup of lemon juice into the same bowl. Now put one small piece of fish into the bowl. Put the second small piece of fish on a plate. Wait 8 minutes and use a spoon to remove the fish from the bowl.

Smell the lemon-coated fish. Use a spoon to remove the fish from the plate. Smell this plain, dry fish. Which piece of fish has a stronger fishy odor?

Old fish smells fishy because amines are released. Amines are molecules that contain nitrogen atoms and often have a bad odor. Amine molecules include a nitrogen atom with either attached hydrogen atoms (NH_2) or hydrocarbon groups (see Figure 23). The amine molecules in fish can go into the air. After they reach your nose and olfactory nerves, you detect a fishy smell.

Lemon juice contains citric acid. Citric acid, like other acids, can give up positive hydrogen atoms (H^+). A positive hydrogen atom can become attached to the amine's nitrogen

Figure 23. Neutral trimethylamine, or C_3H_9N, can gain an H^+ from an acid and become the positive $C_3H_{10}N^+$. Neutral trimethylamine goes in the air and gives a "fishy" smell. However, the charged molecule $C_3H_{10}N^+$ tends to stay in water and on the fish so there is less "fishy" smell in the air.

atom causing molecule–NH_2 to become molecule–NH_3^+, or molecule–N to become molecule–N^+ (see Figure 23). When the amine has a positive charge, it tends to stay in water and on the surface of the fish. Since the charged amine molecules do not go into the air, they cannot reach your nose. When lemon juice is added to fish, you will not detect a strong fishy odor, and it tastes better.

When fish is allowed to rot or when fish is gutted, it releases enzymes that break down protein molecules. When the protein molecules break down, amine molecules such as trimethylamine (C_3H_9N) are formed. Amines produced by spoiled fish can make people sick so it is important to eat fish that has been kept cold or frozen.

Other bad-smelling amines include cadaverine and putrescine, which are released from rotting flesh. As you could guess, both of these amines have disgusting odors. Small amounts of both are sometimes found in bad breath.

Project Idea and Further Investigation

Try repeating this experiment with 5 pieces of fish using 5 different mixtures of water and lemon juice. Use pure water; 1/4 water and 3/4 lemon juice; 1/2 water and 1/2 lemon juice; 3/4 water and 1/4 lemon juice; and pure lemon juice. Have several people smell each piece of fish and rank the fish from most to least smelly. On a graph, plot the strength of the fishy smell versus the amount of lemon juice.

Further Reading

Atkins, Peter W. *Molecules*. New York: W. H. Freeman and Company, 1987.

Branzei, Sylvia. *Virtual Grossology*. Reading, Mass.: Addison-Wesley Publishing Co., 1997.

Cobb, Vicki. *More Science Experiments You Can Eat*. New York: HarperCollins Publishers, 1995.

Grosser, Arthur E. *The Cookbook Decoder or Culinary Alchemy Explained*. New York: Warner Books, 1981.

Hickman, Pamela, and illustrated by Pat Stephens. *Animal Senses: How Animals See, Hear, Taste, Smell, and Feel*. Buffalo, N.Y.: Kids Can Press Ltd., 1998.

Lawless, Julia. *The Illustrated Encyclopedia of Essential Oils*. Boston, Mass.: Element Books Ltd., 1995.

Llamas, Andreu, and illustrated by Francisco Arredondo. *Smell*. New York: Chelsea House Publishers, 1996.

Santa Fe Writers Group. *Bizarre & Beautiful Noses*. Santa Fe, N.M.: John Muir Publications, 1993.

Schiller, David, and Carol Schiller. *Aromatherapy Basics*. New York: Sterling Publishing Co., 1998.

Wildwood, Chrissie. *The Encyclopedia of Aromatherapy*. Rochester, Vt.: Healing Arts Press, 1996.

Pamphlets listed below may be purchased from the Sense of Smell Institute, 145 East 32nd Street, New York, N.Y. 10016:

Living Well with Your Sense of Smell. New York: Olfactory Research Fund, Ltd., 1992.

The Fragrance & Olfactory Dictionary. New York: The Fragrance Foundation and Olfactory Research Fund, Ltd., 1994.

Internet Addresses

A.C. Noble's Homepage of Sensory Science.
http://wineserver.ucdavis.edu/acnoble/home.html
(Flavor wheels are available here.)

Chudler, Eric. H. *Neuroscience for Kids.* "The Senses." © 1996–2001.
http://faculty.washington.edu/chudler/chsense.html

Florida State University Neuroscience Program. *The Vomeronasal Organ.*
http://neuro.fsu.edu/research/vomer.htm

Howard Hughes Medical Institute. *Seeing, Hearing, and Smelling the World.* © 1997. http://www.hhmi.org/senses

Jacob, Tim. *Olfaction.*
http://www.cf.ac.uk/biosi/staff/jacob/teaching/sensory/olfact1.html

Leffingwell and Associates. *Olfaction.* © 1999–2001.
http://www.leffingwell.com/olfaction.htm

National Institute on Deafness and Other Communication Disorders. Health Information. *Because You Asked About Smell and Taste Disorders.* http://www.nidcd.nih.gov/health/pubs_st/smltaste.htm

Sense of Smell Institute. http://www.senseofsmell.org

Society for Neuroscience. *Brain Briefings.* "Smell and the Olfactory System." © 1995. http://www.sfn.org/briefings/smell.html

Spangler, Fredrick A. *The ChemoReception Web.*
http://www.csa.com/crw/home.html

The University of Tennessee at Chattanooga. *The William H. Wheeler Center for Odor Research.* © 2000. http://www.utc.edu/~wheeler

Full use of the sites listed below requires downloading the plugin "Chime" from **http://www.mdlchime.com/chime** from MDL Information Systems Inc. These sites allow you to view and rotate models of odor molecules.

Cornell University. © 1997. *Flavornet.* http://www.nysaes.cornell.edu/fst/faculty/acree/flavornet/index.html

University of California Regents. *ChemConnections.* "Smell Database." © 1995–2000. http://mc2.cchem.berkeley.edu/Smells/index.html

Index